·COMPUTER CLUB·

ROBOTS

Text:
David Harrison

Programs:
Steve Wallace

Macdonald

A MACDONALD BOOK

© Macdonald & Co (Publishers) 1985

First published in Great Britain in 1985
by Macdonald & Co (Publishers) Ltd
London & Sydney

A BPCC plc Company

ISBN 0 356 11023 0

Printed and bound in Belgium
by Henri Proost

Macdonald & Co (Publishers) Ltd
Maxwell House
74 Worship Street
London EC2A 2EN

Series editor
Daphne Butler

Book editor
Donna Bailey

Production
Rosemary Bishop

Picture Research
Kathy Lockley

Consultants
Derrick Daines
John Billingsley

Teacher Panel
John Allen
Vernon Beaumont

Book Design
Richard Garratt

Illustrators
Keith Duran
Linden Artists
Brian Watson
Paula Youens

Photographs
Aldus Archive   7
Austin Rover   8, 24BL
BBC Photographs *Front cover*
Colne Robotics   39
Commotion   15B
Fiat Auto (UK) Ltd/M. Thorold-Palmer   24BR
Gadgets Restaurant & Bar, Gadgets Cafe   32T, 32BR
Jerome Hamlin, ComRo Inc   17T
Lamberton Robotics   24BR
Lucas Film Ltd   4
McAndroids Ltd   32L
Musée d'Art et d'Histoire, Neuchatel   33R, 33L
NASA   34, 34–5
N.Y.P.L. Billy Rose Theatre Collection   4–5
N.Y.P.L. Picture Collection   5B
Jim Pickerell Associates   24TL
Prism Consumer Products   16R
R.B. Robot Corp.   17B
Unimation (Europe) Ltd   25TR
Valiant Designs   15T
ZEFA   10
Zenith Data Systems Ltd   16L

Acknowledgements
For help and advice to
Portsmouth Polytechnic
Barclaycard Ltd

British Library Cataloguing Data
Harrison, David, *1951–*
    Robots.—(Computer club)
    1. Robots—Data processing—Juvenile literature
    2. Microcomputers—Juvenile literature
    I. Title   II. Series
    629.8'92   TJ211.2

ISBN 0-356-11023-0

About this book

There are three different ways in which you can use this book. One way is to use it to find out more about robotics. A second way is to use the programs and information to carry out robot projects with a microcomputer. The third way is to use the programs to develop your computer skills. Projects for the computer are on pages with a blue border. Each project is positioned in the book next to robot information needed for the program.

About the programs

The programs are written in structured BASIC for the BBC microcomputer, and are designed to be changed and adapted. Each project page has a description of the program, a listing of the program, and suggestions for changes you can make.

Start by reading the description and then type the program in at the keyboard of your computer. The program must be copied exactly. It is very likely that you will make mistakes and before the program will run it must be debugged.

When the program is running properly you can use it as part of a robot project. You can also try out the program changes suggested after the program listing. Perhaps you can invent your own modifications.

The programs can be saved on disc or cassette, copied, and given to your friends, but under no circumstances may you sell them.

A cassette tape containing the programs in this book is available for the BBC Model B and the Spectrum 48k.

For the absolute beginner

Before trying to use the programs please get a knowledgeable adult or friend to teach you the following things:

How to use the keyboard.
How to type in and run a program.
How to save a program on cassette tape or disc.
How to load a program from cassette tape or disc.

ROBOTS

Contents

★Pages containing computer programs, data,
or hints for using your microcomputer
are enclosed in stars★

Mechanical men

▲ This scene from Karel Capek's play, RUR, shows the robot slaves overpowering their master. The robots have decided that he is an imperfect being and must be destroyed.

◄ A more friendly image of robots was presented by R2D2 and CP3O in the film Star Wars.

Hero of Alexandria was a Greek mathematician and inventor who lived in the 1st century AD. He designed many hydraulically operated statues. This drawing shows Hercules striking a dragon, which then spits water at him. ▶

What is a robot? We still think of robots as metal imitations of humans, with steel claws for hands, but today's robots are really 'computers with muscles'. Computers can make machines more intelligent. They enable machines to sense and react to our world. It is because these machines seem almost alive that they remind us of robots in stories and films.

Fictional robots have grown out of an age old fascination with gadgets that look 'alive'. As long ago as 1500 BC the Egyptians were making water clocks with moving figures which struck the hours. Most animated figures were made to amuse rich patrons or royalty. Their popularity reached a peak in the eighteenth century, when they were common in the courts of Europe. They were powered by clockwork and had very intricate mechanisms. Two of the best examples were a steel spider that crawled about, and a moving snake that could hiss and spit.

These robot ancestors were known as automata. The word 'robot' did not appear until 1922. It comes from the Czech word 'Robotnik' meaning slave, and was first used in a play called 'Rossum's Universal Robots'.

With the coming of the industrial revolution in the 1790s, the machine began to lose its mystery. The technological achievements of railways and electric light often seemed more fantastic than automata. People's imaginations turned to stories of what machines might be like in the future. The story of Frankenstein, written in 1818, raised questions about how people might be threatened by machines which had free will. These questions fascinated people and became the basis of science fiction.

Some films now feature friendly robots as we are more used to living with machines.

Machines or many hands?

Before the industrial revolution, work was done with human muscle and sweat. Most people laboured on the land, growing food and tending cattle. Their bodies converted the food they ate into muscle power. Power from muscles, not machines, was used to cultivate the land. Jobs like ploughing and harvesting required many hours of work. Horses were used to pull the ploughs and carts, but almost all other work was done by hand. People worked from dawn to dusk just to have enough to eat.

The industrial revolution brought great changes to the way people lived and worked. The steam engine provided a source of power for machines of many types. It converted energy stored in coal into power to drive machinery. This machinery could do the work of many hands.

A revolution is a violent change, an overturning of the old way of doing things, and it was some time before the benefits of the change could be understood. Manufactured goods had been traditionally made by hand by villagers, but the new machines could make and spin and weave more efficiently. People flocked from the countryside to work with the machines because wages

6

were higher. However the factories were unpleasant and sometimes dangerous places to work in, and the homes in the manufacturing towns that grew up around them were often badly built.

With the invention of more and more machines, the need for labour in the form of muscle power declined. These machines needed people to operate them, and so new jobs were created. With the industrial revolution, the human role changed from being a source of power for

◄ *When James Watt introduced his revolutionary new steam engine in 1769, enormous advances were made in the development of power for factories and workshops.*

Machines have also revolutionised work on the land, so that large areas of wheat can now be harvested with the help of only two or three combine harvesters. ►

labour into being a controller of machines. Today we are facing a second revolution, as machines tended by people are increasingly being replaced by computer controlled robots.

▲ *Before the industrial revolution people worked mainly on the land. The invention of machines meant most people started to work in factories, and gradually leisure time increased. In the future people may transact business and do the shopping without leaving their homes.*

Computers in control

Some of the machines designed during the industrial revolution did not need people to look after them but had their own control mechanisms. Perhaps the simplest controller was the governor used to help a steam engine run at a constant speed. It disconnected the engine if it went too fast, and reconnected it as it slowed down. In this way it behaved as a mechanical valve.

A computer could be used to control a steam engine, but it would work electrically, not mechanically like the governor. Computers control by processing information. They link signals from sensors with instructions which are stored in the computer's memory. Using sensors to monitor the steam pressure, a computer could adjust a control valve to the correct level. Similarly, to control a washing machine, a computer must keep track of all the important goings on: the temperature of the water, the rate of water flow, and the number of revolutions of the drum.

Computers offer more flexible control than the mechanisms they replace, and are used in everyday machines from sewing machines to toasters and videos. The older controllers used clockwork to make things happen at certain times, like a twenty minute wash followed by a five minute rinse. To allow for more choice, like a twenty-five minute wash for extra dirty clothes, would have required more clockwork and would have cost more. If you substitute a computer controller, this kind of option can be programmed in the computer's software. No extra moving parts are required, except perhaps another button to tell the computer you have extra dirty socks!

Computers on the road

Computers do useful work under the bonnet of many cars. They control the engine efficiently and reduce the amount of exhaust pollution. Some cars also have computers on the dashboard which work out fuel consumption or advise the driver of the external temperature and the condition of the road surface. More useful is a prototype car with a computer which can tell the driver the best route to his destination. It receives information on traffic conditions via cables in the road and works out the best route to avoid hold-ups. The car's computer then draws a map on its screen for the driver to follow.

This modern car control panel includes not only the usual instruments, but also signals whether doors are properly closed and provides warning about problems or defects in the engine. ▼

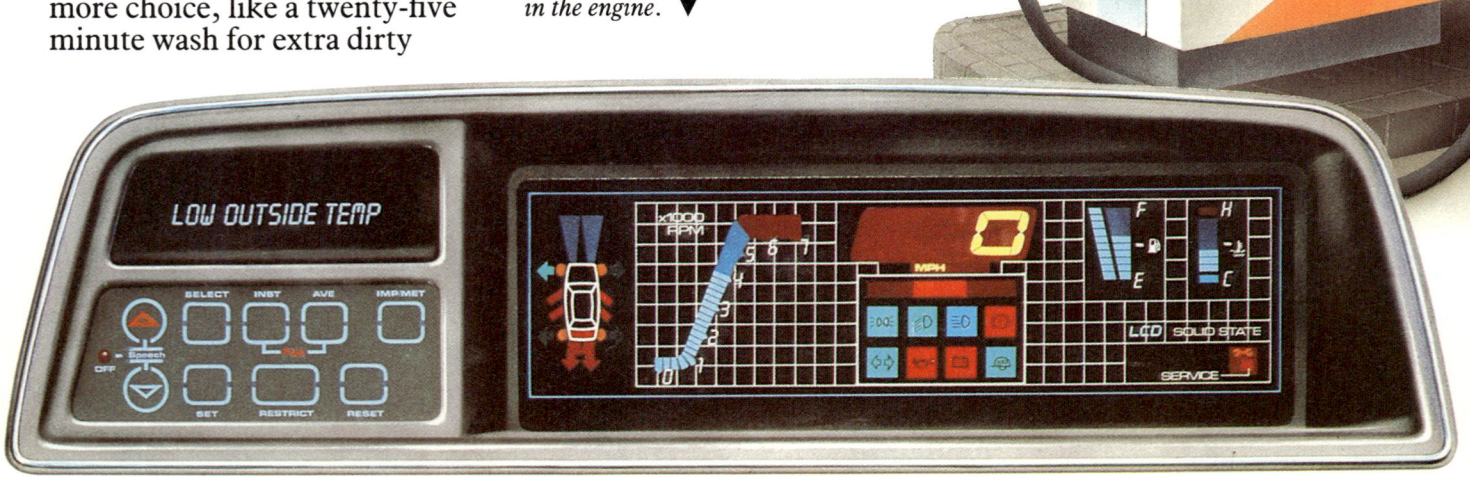

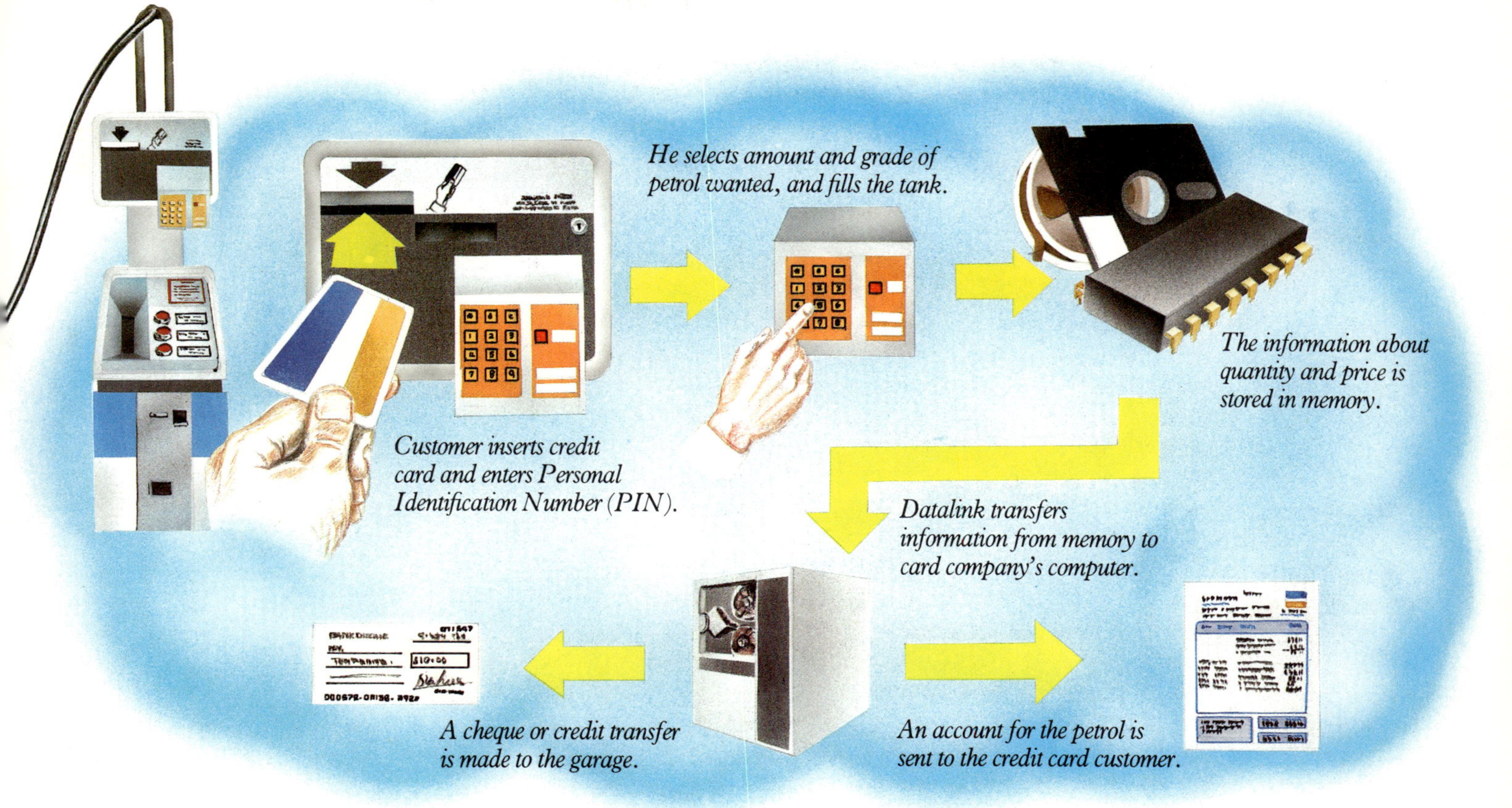

He selects amount and grade of petrol wanted, and fills the tank.

Customer inserts credit card and enters Personal Identification Number (PIN).

The information about quantity and price is stored in memory.

Datalink transfers information from memory to card company's computer.

An account for the petrol is sent to the credit card customer.

A cheque or credit transfer is made to the garage.

▲ Some petrol pumps are controlled by computers, allowing automatic payment by credit card and a 24 hour service.

The driver information system is backed up by a voice synthesis unit, which warns the driver about fastening seatbelts or needing more petrol.

The ignition system is programmed to be fully automatic with a 'thinking carburettor'.

▲ Modern car assembly uses the latest generation of highly flexible automation and robotics. Body shells are brought together on automated assembly lines, and finished in the paint plant, where paints and finishes are applied by robots. Robots insert the windscreens and check the fascia, the car's entire electrical system and the automatic tyre fitment.

External sensors monitor the temperature and warn the driver of frost and ice on the road.

Electronic sensors assist the driver to park by warning him, on a visual display unit, of the distances to the nearest objects.

Robots for reliability

We have seen how computers can do useful work by controlling special machines. Given arms and hands, a computer can do more varied physical work. With a robot 'body', a computer 'brain' may be programmed to pick up tools and parts and move them around.

The ability to work under the control of a program is what distinguishes robots from less 'intelligent' machines. Cranes and mechanical diggers can pick up things and move them around, but they are not robots. These machines need men to drive and control them; they cannot be controlled by a program like a true robot.

Computers are very reliable; they can work for a long time without breaking down. This is because they have no moving parts. Robots need lots of moving parts. They have motors and gearboxes which move and can wear out, and they need people to maintain them like any other machine. Eventually robots will probably be able to service and mend each other. However, robots are generally predictable, precise and untiring in their work. Used correctly they can improve the quality of products, as they do not have 'off' days. They can also bring savings in materials and energy.

Human workers now have the number of hours they work each day limited by law. The law also protects them from working in dangerous conditions. In special factories robots can work happily for 24 hours a day. They work on through the night while their human supervisors are at home in bed. If there were any problems, the robots could ring up the supervisor and ask for help!

This factory in Japan shows people employed in making watches. These days, robots are increasingly being used for manufacturing precision instruments. ▶

Robots for factories are expensive, costing thousands of U.S. dollars. The high cost is slowing down their introduction into industry and moderating their effects. They will continue to displace workers from dangerous and repetitive jobs. For example in some car factories, robots are being used to assemble car bonnets. The glueing and pressing of bonnets used to involve two people in very unpleasant work. A robot has been introduced which can apply the glue. It can apply the glue consistently and the cost of each bonnet is reduced as only one man is required to assemble it.

Many supermarkets have semi-automated, computer controlled systems, reducing the number of people employed in the warehouse.

Stock on the shelves in the supermarket is checked by the use of a wand which reads the bar codes printed on the goods. This gives information to the computer about the product. At the check-out tills, lasers read the same information as the cashier passes each item over a scanning window. The information from both these sources is passed to the supermarket's stock control computer.

When more goods of a certain item are required the information is passed to the warehouse computer, which orders the goods from the supplier. On arrival the

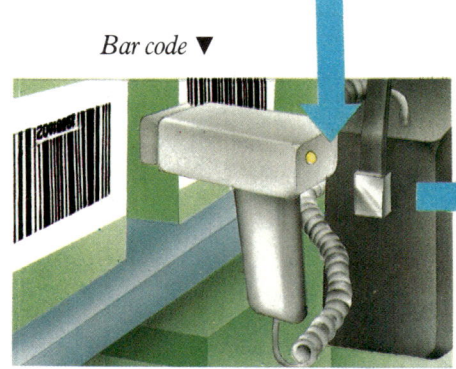

Bar code ▼

goods are stored by robot stacker-cranes in a high-bay storage area.

The robot cranes load and unload the goods from automatic trolleys, which take the goods to the supermarket's delivery vans. The vans deliver the goods to the stockroom at the supermarket, and when required, the goods are placed on the shelves by the assistants. ▶

*Stock control
computer* ▼

▲ *Supermarket*

*Supermarket
stock room* ▼

Automatic warehouse ▼

▲ *Warehouse computer*

▼ *Loading bay*

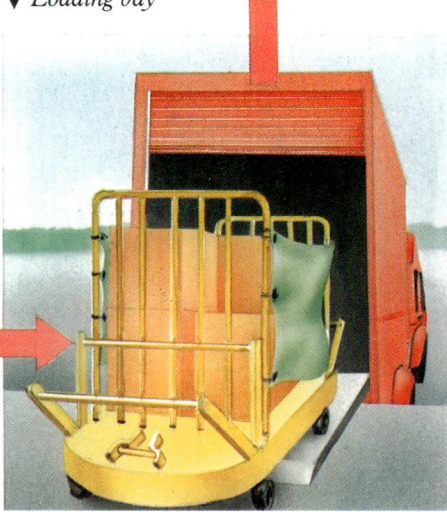

Program:
MINDREAD

This is a 'Think of a number' game. The computer will ask you to think of a number and ask you to change that number in four simple ways. Then you type in your result and, after a magic mind-reading display, the computer will tell you the number you first thought of. Is it magic? At first it looks as if it might be, but actually it's algebra!

Type the program into your computer and debug it so that it runs properly. Save the program on cassette.

```
 10 MODE2
 20 VDU 23,1,0;0;0;0;
 30 *FX11,0
 40 COLOUR 11
 50 PRINT TAB(0,10)"**The mind reading
** "
 60 PRINT"    **Computer**"
 70 COLOUR 2
 80 PRINT TAB(2,20)"Sound? Yes or No"
 90 Z=GET
100 IF Z=89 THEN sound=1 ELSE sound=0
110 CLS:COLOUR 11
120 PRINT TAB(2,5)"Think of a number"
130 COLOUR 2
140 PRINT TAB(0,12)"Write it down on"´
´"paper.This time YOU"´´"can do the sums
!"
150 PROCwait("A")


160 COLOUR 11 :REM Call the number X
170 PRINT TAB(4,10)"Now double it"
180 REM Now we have 2X
190 PROCwait("B")


200 PRINT TAB(4,10)"Now add four"
210 REM 2x+4
220 PROCwait("C")


230 PRINT TAB(2,10)"Now divide by two"
240 REM (2X+4)/2=X+2
250 PROCwait("D")


260 PRINT TAB(2,10)"Now add thirteen"
270 REM X+2+13=X+15
280 PROCwait("E")
```

```
290 *FX21,0
300 PRINT TAB(1,10)"Type in your resul
t"
310 FOR wait=0 TO 1500:NEXT wait
320 COLOUR 2
330 INPUT TAB(2,14)"Then press"´´"   RE
TURN   "Y
340 PROCdisplay
350 COLOUR 2
360 *FX21,0
370 PRINT TAB(0,10)"Your original numb
erwas "´´Y-15
380 PRINT TAB(0,20)"Another go? Y/N"
390 IF GET$<>"N" THEN RUN
400 VDU 23,1,1;0;0;0;
410 *FX12,0
420 COLOUR 128:CLS:PRINT TAB(6,10)"Goo
dbye":END


430 DEF PROCwait(A$)
440 COLOUR 2
450 PRINT TAB(4,25)"Then press "A$
460 IF GET$<>A$ THEN 460
470  IF sound=1 THEN VDU 7 ELSE GOTO 4
80
480 CLS:COLOUR 11
490 ENDPROC


500 DEF PROCdisplay
510 FOR X=1TO7
520   ENVELOPE 1,7,2,1,1,1,1,1,121,-10
,-5,-2,120,120
530   COLOUR 128+X:CLS
540   FOR N=1 TO 8
550     SOUND 2,sound,RND(255),2
560     NEXT N
570   NEXT X
580 COLOUR 128:CLS
590 ENDPROC
```

Hint
When playing the game make sure your sums are right before you type in the answer. If you get the arithmetic wrong so will the computer.

What next?
Once you understand how the trick works try designing your own 'Think of a number' game using different algebra. You will need to change lines 170 to 330 and line 370.

This program helps you to design a colourful repeating pattern. There are two stages to the program. First you must decide which shapes to use. You can choose up to six shapes from a choice of ten. Each shape can be coloured. There are ten colours to choose from including black and two flashing colours. Once you have designed your row of coloured shapes the computer repeats the pattern until it fills the screen.

Type the program into your computer and debug it so that it runs properly. Save the program on cassette.

```
 10 MODE 2
 20 VDU 23,1,0;0;0;0;
 30 PROCinitialise
 40 PROCdesign:PROCdisplay
 50 *FX21,0
 60 PRINT TAB(0,33)"Another go? Y/N"
 70 Z=GET
 80 IF Z=89 OR Z=121 THEN 40
 90 CLS:VDU 23,1,1;0;0;0;
100 PRINT TAB(6,10)"Goodbye":END

110 DEF PROCinitialise
120 DIMchar(6):DIMcol(6)
130 VDU 23,240,15,15,15,15,240,240,240
,240
140 VDU 23,241,240,240,240,240,15,15,1
5,15
150 VDU 23,242,15,15,15,15,255,255,255
,255
160 VDU 23,243,240,240,240,240,255,255
,255,255
170 VDU 23,244,255,255,255,255,240,240
,240,240
180 VDU 23,245,255,255,255,255,15,15,1
5,15
190 VDU 23,246,24,60,126,255,255,126,6
0,24
200 VDU 23,247,195,231,102,24,24,102,2
31,195
210 VDU 23,248,240,240,240,240,240,240
,240,240
220 VDU 23,249,0,0,0,0,15,15,15,15
230 VDU 19,8,12,0,0,0
240 ENDPROC

250 DEF PROCspace
260 COLOUR 7:COLOUR 128
270 PRINT TAB(0,23)STRING$(80," ")
280 VDU 11,11,11,11
290 ENDPROC

300 DEF PROCdesign
310 CLS:COLOUR 7
320 PRINT TAB(1,1)"Make a row of up to
"
330 PRINT TAB(5,3)"six shapes"
340 PROCpalette
350 VDU 17,128:PROCspace
360 PRINT" How long will your"
370 INPUT´" row be ?"length
380 IF length>6 GOTO 350
390 PROCspace
400 FOR ct=1 TO length
410    PROCspace
420    PRINT "Shape number ";ct;" is ";
430    INPUT S
440    IF S<1 OR S>10 THEN GOTO 410
450    char(ct)=S+239
460    PRINT TAB(ct,29)CHR$(char(ct))
470    PROCspace
480    INPUT"Which colour?"S
490    IF S>9 THEN GOTO 470
500    col(ct)=S
510    COLOUR S
520    PRINT TAB(ct,29)CHR$(char(ct))
530    NEXT ct
540 wait=INKEY(100)
550 ENDPROC

560 DEF PROCdisplay
570 CLS:print=0
580 REPEAT
590    FOR ct=1 TO length
600       COLOUR col(ct)
610       PRINT CHR$(char(ct));
620       print=print+1
630    NEXT ct
640    UNTIL print=600
650 COLOUR 2
660 ENDPROC

670 DEF PROCpalette
680 GCOL0,2:COLOUR 2
690 MOVE 0,880:DRAW 1280,880
700 MOVE 0,368:DRAW 1280,368
710 PRINT TAB(1,5)"Choose from these"
720 PRINT´" shapes and colours"
730 PRINT´´"1 2 3 4 5 6 7 8 9 10"
740 VDU 17,7,240,9,241,9,242,9,243,9,2
44,9,245,9,246,9,247,9,248,9,249,13,10,1
0,10
750 COLOUR 2
760 PRINT"0 1 2 3 4 5 6 7 8 9 "
770 FOR ct=0 TO 9
780    COLOUR ct+128:VDU 32,9
790    NEXT ct
800 ENDPROC
```

Beasties, buggies and turtles

The first electronic turtle was built by Gray Walter in 1957. It ran around the floor, and would make off in the other direction if it bumped into furniture, but was attracted to light. Its workings were very simple; it had a photo-electric sensor coupled to its steering which took it towards a source of bright light. When the turtle's shell came into contact with anything, the pressure activated a switch which reversed the turtle motor, backing it away from the obstacle.

Turtles connected to microcomputers are now popular in schools. You can program instructions into the computer and watch the turtle obey, and draw pictures on the floor under the control of a program you have written.

Buggies are little cars which can be controlled by your home computer. Equipped with touch and simple vision sensors, they can explore the world around the computer. They can be programmed to follow a line or track down a light source, like Gray Walter's turtle. Some have programs that allow them to search for an object using their touch sensors, to trace round its outline, and to draw its shape on the computer screen.

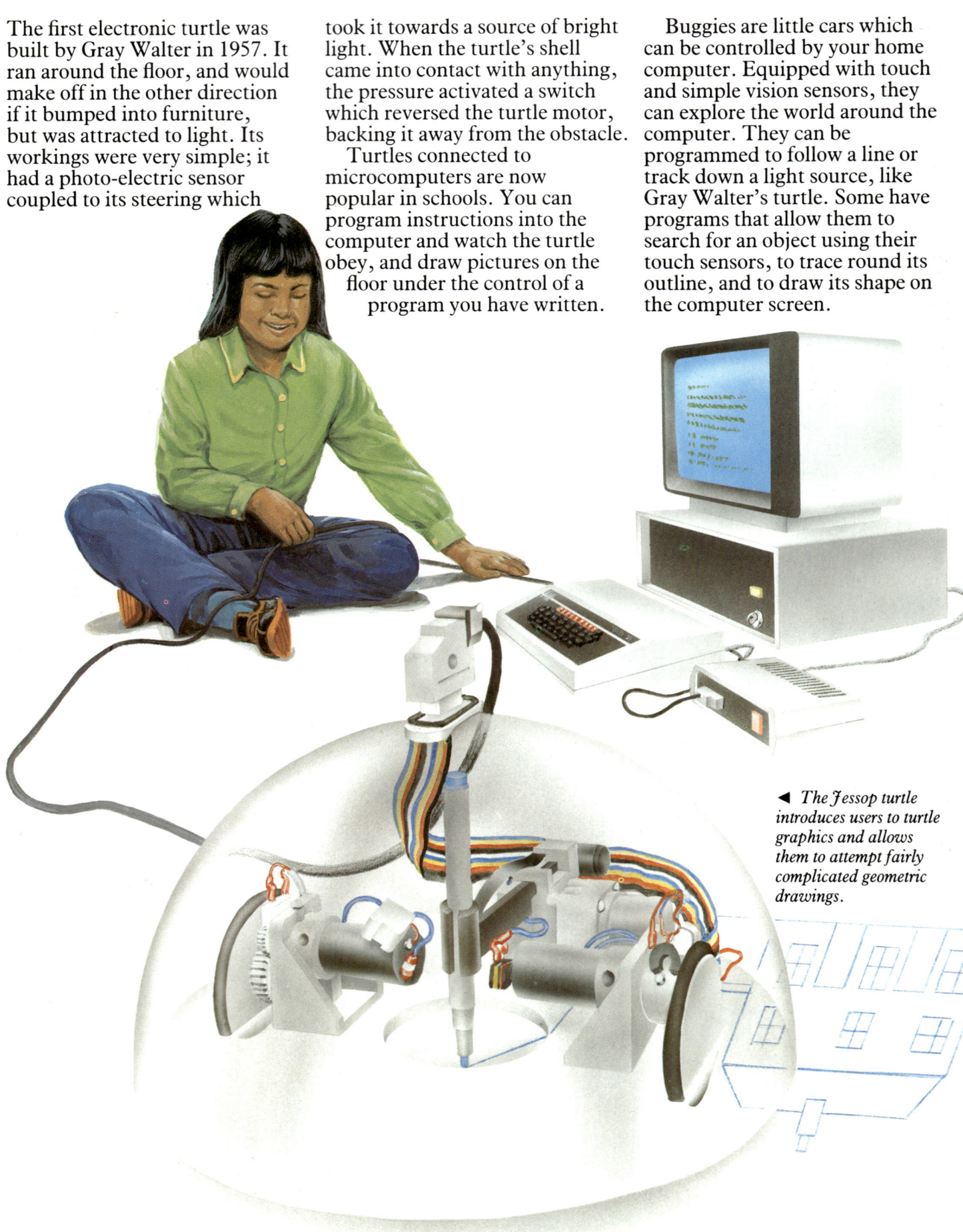

◀ *The Jessop turtle introduces users to turtle graphics and allows them to attempt fairly complicated geometric drawings.*

The Valiant turtle is controlled by an infra-red remote control link. A small transmitter is attached to the computer, and its signals are picked up by the turtle. It is controlled by a program based on a computer language called LOGO which controls the turtle's movements, and enables it to draw arcs, circles and triangles. ▶

If you are interested in building your own robot arm, then Beasties are for you. They are small rugged units that allow direct control of servo motors by a home computer. Servo is another word meaning slave, and these motors are known as servo motors as they obey commands from the computer. Using the computer and a servo amplifier like the Beastie, you can command the motor shaft to rotate to a position of your choice. If a number of these motors are connected together with an arm framework, each one becomes a robot joint. The commands to the motors from the computer can now control the position of the end of the arm, just like a real robot.

The Beastie is a small black box, which can control up to four servo mechanisms through a computer program called ROBOL. A robot arm can be attached to the Beastie, allowing it to lift, twist, open, close and pick up objects such as this camera, under computer control. ▶

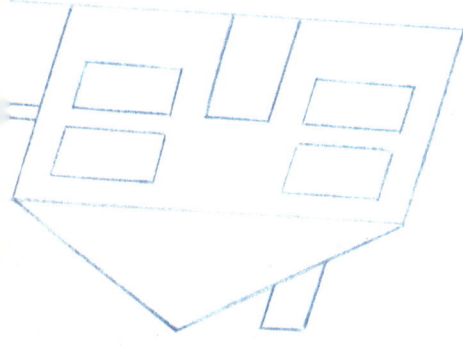

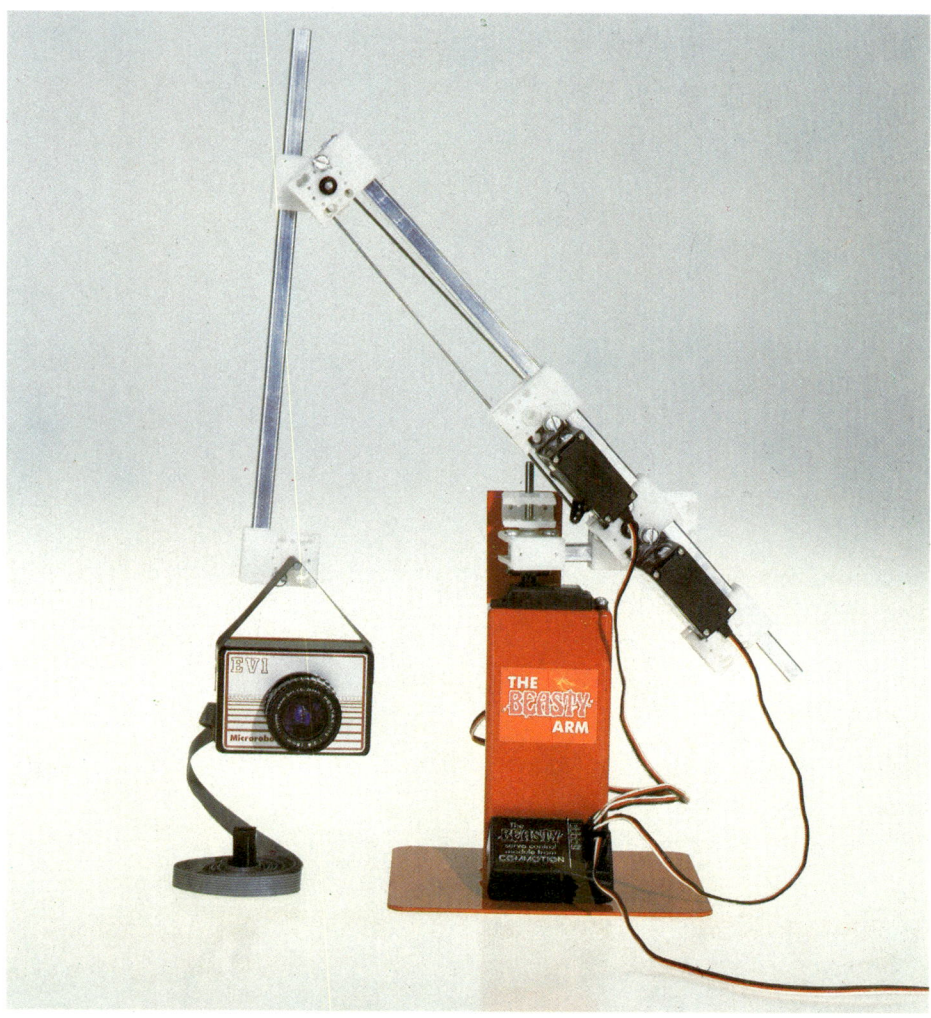

Personal robots

Servants of the future?

The idea of having a robot as a domestic servant is not new, but the personal robots that are available today are of little use. Chores like washing up and making beds are well beyond all of them.

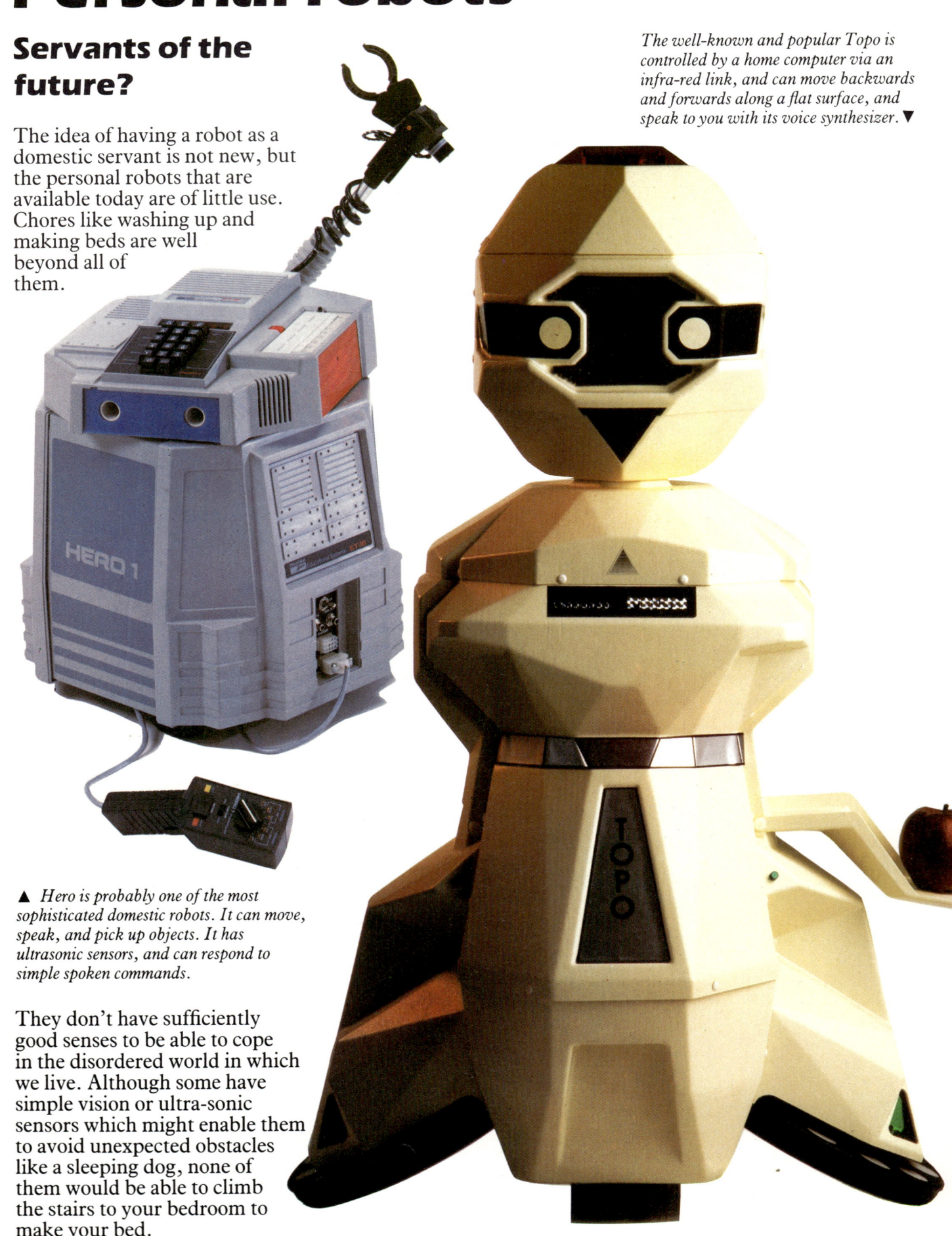

The well-known and popular Topo is controlled by a home computer via an infra-red link, and can move backwards and forwards along a flat surface, and speak to you with its voice synthesizer. ▼

▲ *Hero is probably one of the most sophisticated domestic robots. It can move, speak, and pick up objects. It has ultrasonic sensors, and can respond to simple spoken commands.*

They don't have sufficiently good senses to be able to cope in the disordered world in which we live. Although some have simple vision or ultra-sonic sensors which might enable them to avoid unexpected obstacles like a sleeping dog, none of them would be able to climb the stairs to your bedroom to make your bed.

There are a number of
personal robots available, but
most are quite similar in
design. They are all upright
and move about on wheels.
Balancing on two legs is actually
very difficult! Most personal
robots are about a metre high,
and look a bit like space-age
coffee tables.

"Forget trying to do anything
serious with them – they should
be treated as things for fun."
That is what Nolan Bushnell,
the 'father' of Topo said about
personal robots. Most of today's
personal robots are valued more
for their entertaining company
than for their usefulness around
the home.

*An important function of home robots is in
security. Tot not only passes drinks, but
will patrol your house using an ultrasonic
sensor to find burglars. Tot can also tell the
time, push a sweeper and carry a bucket.* ▶

▲ *RB5X can sense
objects and turn away,
saying "Excuse me" if it
bumps into you. It is
capable of a number of
actions, including
bringing your slippers.*

Sensors

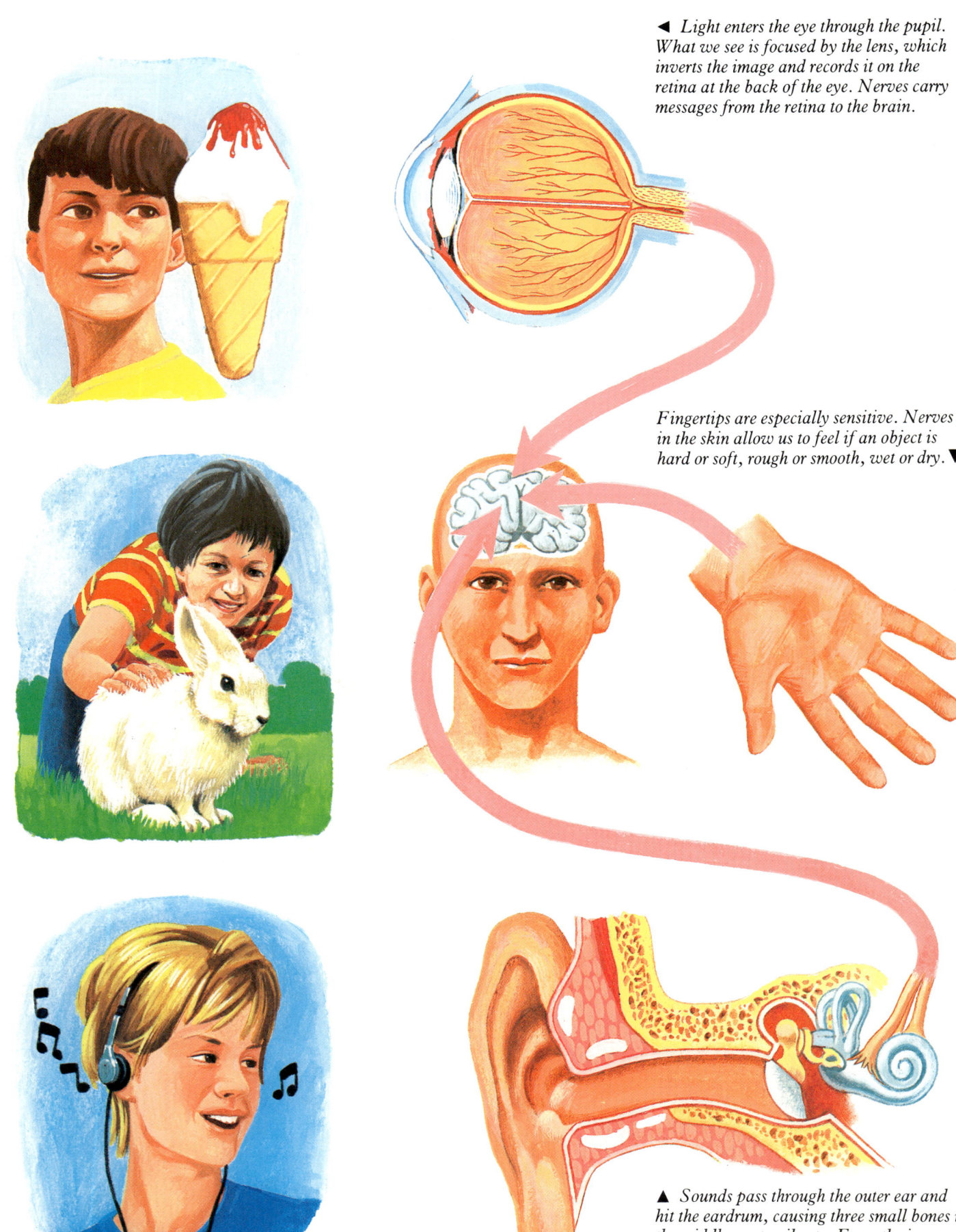

◀ Light enters the eye through the pupil. What we see is focused by the lens, which inverts the image and records it on the retina at the back of the eye. Nerves carry messages from the retina to the brain.

Fingertips are especially sensitive. Nerves in the skin allow us to feel if an object is hard or soft, rough or smooth, wet or dry. ▼

▲ Sounds pass through the outer ear and hit the eardrum, causing three small bones in the middle ear to vibrate. From the inner ear, nerves send messages to the brain.

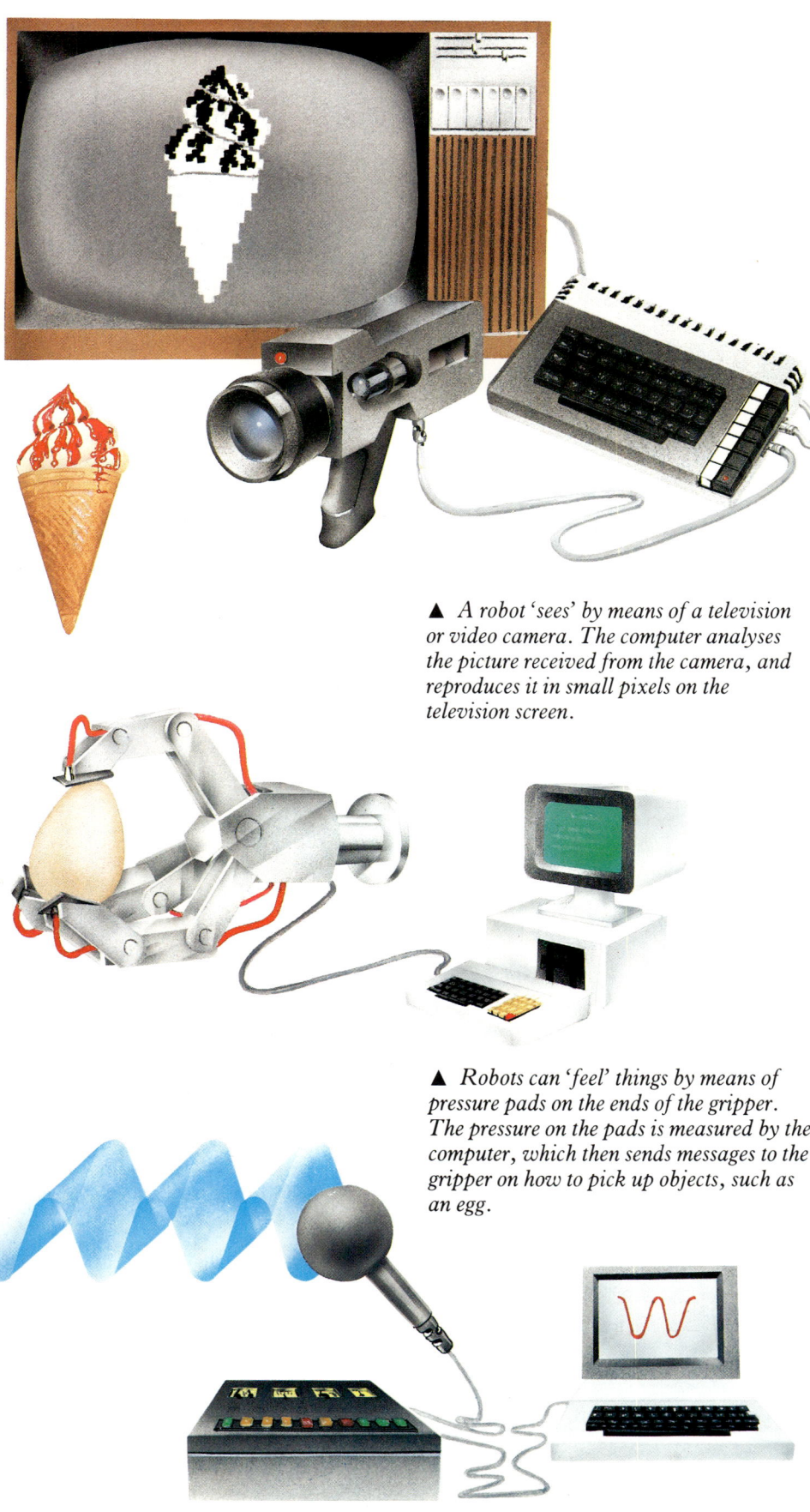

Like humans, robots need sensors to gain information about their surroundings. Robot sensors change patterns in light and sound into electrical signals which can be processed by a computer.

The simplest sensor for robot vision is a single photo-electric cell. This is a tiny piece of material whose electrical properties are dependent on the amount of light falling on it. By looking at how much electric current is flowing through the cell, the computer can tell whether its eye is looking at light or dark.

These sensors are small and only tell the robot about the light falling on a limited area. A number of them may be combined in an array to cover a larger area. The robot can then study the shapes formed by the light falling on the array.

To provide vision over a greater area the robot may analyse a television picture from a standard video camera. This picture will contain a lot more information than is obtained from a simple array of photo-cells. However, the robot takes a long time to extract the bits of information of interest from the mass of other information in the picture.

The noises we hear are vibrations of air falling on our eardrums, which are converted into nerve impulses. These impulses are then passed to the brain where they become sound patterns. In a similar way, robots use a microphone to convert sound into electrical signals.

Touch is another important sense for robots, as much of their work involves picking things up. Most robots use special rubber pads to monitor the pressure on their fingertips. The electrical properties of the rubber change as it is compressed, and the robot's computer can measure these changes.

▲ *A robot 'sees' by means of a television or video camera. The computer analyses the picture received from the camera, and reproduces it in small pixels on the television screen.*

▲ *Robots can 'feel' things by means of pressure pads on the ends of the gripper. The pressure on the pads is measured by the computer, which then sends messages to the gripper on how to pick up objects, such as an egg.*

▲ *A robot can 'hear' things by using a microphone to pick up sound waves in the air. The computer analyses the signal.*

Action

All our knowledge of the outside world comes from our senses, but our brain must process the information before we can learn from it or act on it. Similarly the signals from the robot's sensors must be processed by the robot computer. The computer can then send commands to the robot that are influenced by the sensory information.

In the human body, the coordination of all the information from the senses takes place in the central nervous system (the brain and the spinal cord). A stimulus comes in from a sense organ, and a response is produced in the nervous system. This response is then passed to a muscle or gland, which produces action. For example, a ringing telephone sends a stimulus from your ear to your brain, and your brain responds by commanding muscles in your arm to pick up the phone.

A suitably equipped robot could be programmed to respond to this stimulus in a similar way. A microphone would send a signal to the robot computer. The computer would look at the pattern of this signal and compare it with a sound pattern of a telephone ringing stored in its memory. If the two patterns matched, the computer would find its instructions about how to respond to a telephone bell. Following these instructions, the computer would command the robot arm to pick up the receiver.

By using information from the sensors to direct their actions, robots can do more than just repeat the movements they have been taught. Robots using vision sensors can follow the join between two metal plates, and pass a welding torch along it, forming a seam weld. There are even special assembly robots which can use information from force sensors to help them put components together.

This artist's impression of what a robot of the future might look like illustrates some of the functions which are already carried out by robots. ▼

1 The control mechanism is housed in the central box, and contains a computer to receive and relay messages.

2 A microphone picks up sound waves and allows the robot to hear the man's instructions.

3 A voice synthesizer housed in the control box allows the robot to talk to the man, and ask and answer questions.

4 The flexible arm is powered by servo motors and can extend and retract, and move in many directions.

5 The television 'eye' allows the robot to see the apple and judge the distance from it.

6 The gripper mechanism has pressure pads to allow the robot's computer to judge the pressure needed to pick the apple.

This program will give you a taste of what a pattern drawing robot can do. The robot is a 'graphics turtle'. There are two parts to the program. The first part is a demonstration which shows you how the patterns will be drawn, the second part lets you design your own patterns and repeat them around the screen.

Type the program into your computer and debug it so that it runs properly. Save the program on cassette.

Talking to the turtle

The computer will ask you to decide on the length of each line, and then the angle by which you want the line to turn. Suppose you choose an angle of 45°. Then this is what would happen:
1. The computer draws a line the right length.

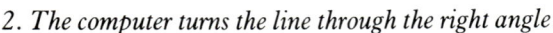

2. The computer turns the line through the right angle.

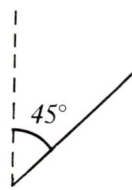

3. The computer repeats the line by turning through your chosen angle.

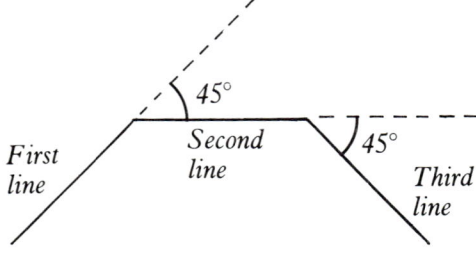

Experiment with different lengths of line, different angles, and different numbers of lines.

Hint

If you want to make a pattern that finishes where it starts (like a square or a triangle) you must do a sum first. Divide the number of sides in the shape into 360. The answer is the correct angle to turn through.

```
  10 MODE 1
  20 PROCinitialise
  30 PROCmenu
  40 PROCend
  50 END


  60 DEF PROCinitialise
  70 VDU 24,0;160;1279;1023;
  80 REM graphics window
  90 VDU 28,0,31,39,27
 100 REM text window
 110 VDU 23,1,0;0;0;0;
 120 REM cursor off
 130 Xcentre=640:Ycentre=640
 140 GCOL 0,128:CLG
 150 VDU 19,1,2,0,0,0
 160 COLOUR 1:CLS
 170 ENDPROC


 180 DEF PROCmenu
 190 REPEAT
 200    CLS
 210    PRINT TAB(7,0)"The pattern
drawing robot"
 220    PRINT TAB(4,1)"1 Demonstrat
ion  2 Make patterns"
 230    PRINT TAB(4,2)"3 Stop"
 240    PRINT TAB(12,3)"Choose 1, 2
 or 3"
 250    Z=GET
 260    IF Z=49 THEN PROCdemo ELSE
IF Z=50 THEN PROCpatterns
 270    UNTIL Z=51
 280 ENDPROC


 290 DEF PROCdemo
 300 time=600
 310 CLS:CLG
 320 length=200:newpos=360
 330 angle=60
 340 sideno=1
 350 PROCdisplay
 360 PRINT"This line is 200 units
long."
 370 PRINT"Now I'll turn through 6
0 degrees and     draw another line
the same.";
 380 PROCwait
 390 sideno=2:PROCdisplay
 400 PRINT"Now I will do that anot
her 4 times."
```

```
 410 PROCwait
 420 sideno=6:PROCdisplay
 430 PRINT"This pattern has six si
des."
 440 PRINT"After each side I turne
d through 60     degrees."
 450 PROCwait
 460 COLOUR 2
 470 PRINT"Now I will draw the who
le pattern 8     times turning thro
ugh 45 degrees after  each  one."
 480 PROCwait
 490 CLG
 500 newpos=45:PROCdisplay
 510 PROCwait
 520 PRINT"In this program you can
 make your own    patterns and repea
t them  just  like    I did."
 530 PROCwait
 540 ENDPROC


 550 DEF PROCpatterns
 560 time=600
 570 length=0:angle=0:sideno=1:new
pos=360
 580 PROCnumbers
 590 PRINT TAB(0,2)"How long will
each line be?"
 600 INPUT "(Try between 50 and 15
0)"length
 610 PROCnumbers
 620 CLG:PROCdisplay
 630 PRINT TAB(0,2)"What angle sha
ll I turn through?"
 640 INPUT"(Up to 360)"angle
 650 PROCnumbers
 660 CLG:PROCdisplay
 670 INPUT TAB(0,2)"How many lines
 shall I draw?"sideno
 680 PROCnumbers
 690 CLG:PROCdisplay
 700 CLS:PRINT"Do you want to repe
at this pattern?     Yes or No"
 710 Z=GET
 720 IF Z<>89 GOTO 790
 730 CLS:PRINT"What angle shall I
turn through to      repeat the pat
tern?"
 740 INPUT"(Upto 360)"newpos
 750 CLS:PRINT"The pattern is bein
g drawn."
 760 PRINT"every ";newpos;" degree
s"

 770 time=5
 780 PROCdisplay
 790 ENDPROC


 800 DEF PROCdisplay
 810 ANGLE=0:times=0
 820 MOVE Xcentre,Ycentre
 830 REPEAT
 840    times=times+1
 850    FOR count=1 TO sideno
 860      ANGLE=ANGLE+angle
 870      Xnew=length*SIN(RAD(ANGLE
))
 880      Ynew=length*COS(RAD(ANGLE
))
 890      GCOL 0,2
 900      PLOT1,Xnew,Ynew
 910      FOR wait=1 TO time: NEXT
wait
 920      NEXT count
 930    ANGLE=times*newpos
 940    FOR wait=1 TO time: NEXT wa
it
 950    UNTIL ANGLE>=360
 960 ENDPROC


 970 DEF PROCwait
 980 COLOUR 3:PRINT TAB(23,3)"Pres
s any key"
 990 Z=GET
1000 COLOUR 1:CLS
1010 ENDPROC


1020 DEF PROCnumbers
1030 COLOUR 3 :CLS
1040 PRINT TAB(0,0)"length=";lengt
h
1050 PRINT TAB(15,0)"angle=";angle
1060 PRINT TAB(30,0)"sides=";siden
o
1070 COLOUR 1
1080 ENDPROC


1090 DEF PROCend
1100 VDU 26
1110 CLS:CLG:PRINT TAB(16,10)"Good
bye"
1120 ENDPROC
```

Industrial robots

Industrial robots have been working away in factories since the early 1960s. Over 40,000 are now employed throughout the world. They don't look much like their science fiction relatives. None have 'heads' or 'legs', very few can 'speak' or 'hear', and only the latest models can 'see' or have a sense of touch. In fact most industrial robots have only one arm.

This is because these robots have developed from gadgets used in factories to transfer parts to and from cutting machines. In the factory, one 'hand' (or gripper), and a simple 'brain' is all that is required to perform many basic tasks.

One reason why industry uses robots is that they are 'flexible' machines. This means that they can be re-programmed to do different jobs, or easily unbolted from the floor and moved around the factory. Robots are selected for their size, strength, reach, accuracy and speed. Not surprisingly the big, strong robots tend to be slower and less accurate. The biggest is the giant

◀ *Robots are used in factories for many jobs. One use is welding metals at high temperatures (left) which can be a dangerous job for people. Another use is gluing together car bodies (bottom left). Some modern cars are made almost entirely by robots (below), as can be seen at the Fiat works in Brentford, England.* ▼

The tiny Puma 260 robot can only lift 0.9 kg, but is extremely flexible in the tasks it can perform, such as application of adhesives, assembly or insertion of small components, inspection for defects, and testing materials. ▶

▲ *The giant Lamberton robot is one of the biggest in the world. It is used in factories where it is necessary to pick up and move heavy or awkward objects of up to 1500 kg, or where a very long reach is required.*

Lamberton robot, used for lifting steel ingots. It dwarfs the tiny Puma 260 which can lift only 0.9 kg, but can repeat its movements to within 0.05 mm.

Robots are at their best when working in areas that are dangerous for people. They are used to handle red hot metal in foundries, and can load and unload heavy presses which could crush a person. They are also used for paint spraying, a job that can damage lungs, and for spot welding. Humans must wear uncomfortable, heavy protective clothing for these jobs, but the robots require little protection.

As the use of robots becomes more widespread, factories in the future will be designed to suit the machines that work in them. Already some robots are hung upside down from the ceiling to weave wiring looms. They can cover a greater working area in this way, and don't seem to mind a bit!

How robots move

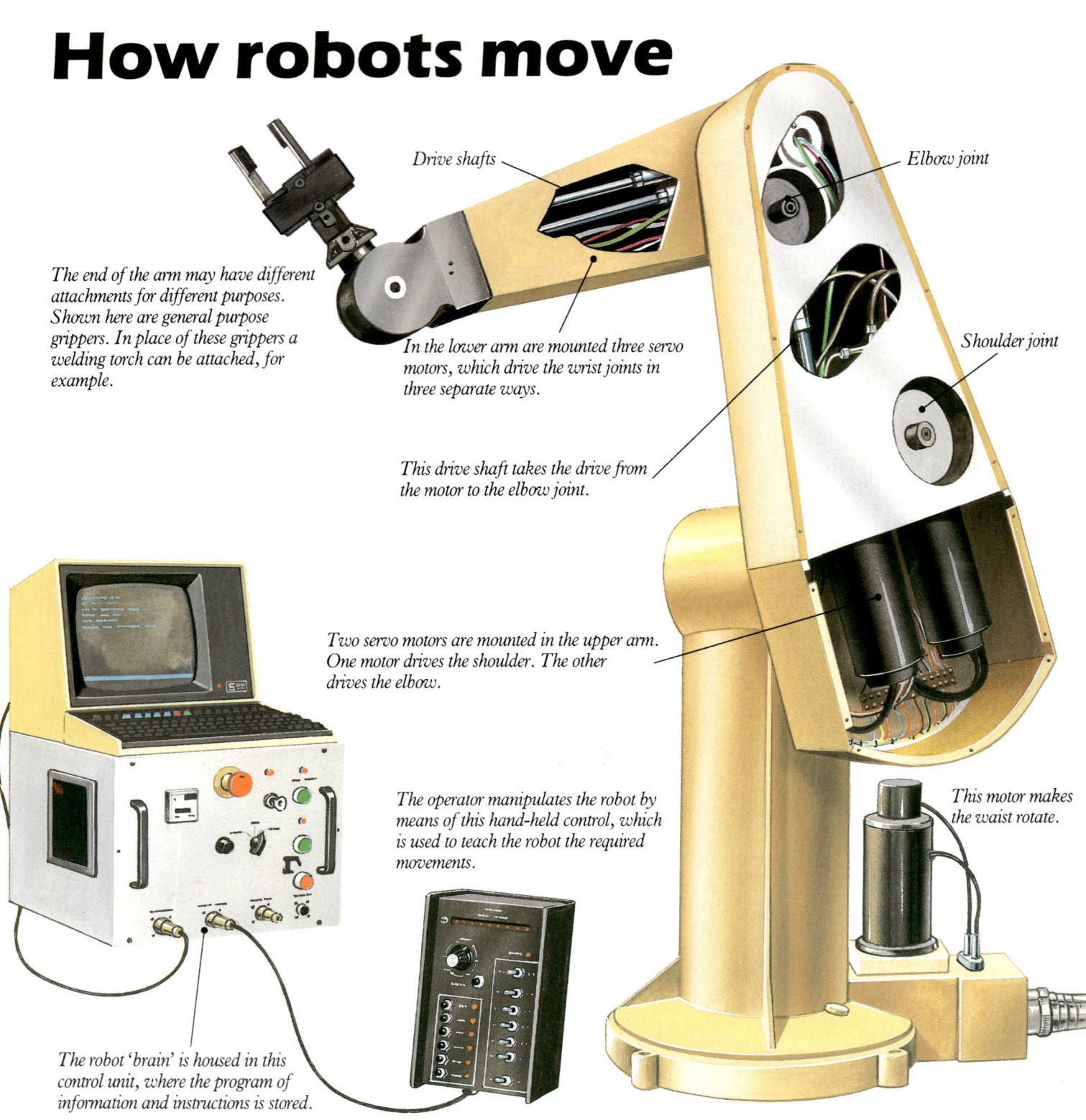

The end of the arm may have different attachments for different purposes. Shown here are general purpose grippers. In place of these grippers a welding torch can be attached, for example.

Drive shafts

In the lower arm are mounted three servo motors, which drive the wrist joints in three separate ways.

This drive shaft takes the drive from the motor to the elbow joint.

Elbow joint

Shoulder joint

Two servo motors are mounted in the upper arm. One motor drives the shoulder. The other drives the elbow.

The operator manipulates the robot by means of this hand-held control, which is used to teach the robot the required movements.

This motor makes the waist rotate.

The robot 'brain' is housed in this control unit, where the program of information and instructions is stored.

All robots are a combination of moving parts and a control system or 'brain'. Although some robots move around on wheels, most industrial robots are fixed. Some have rectangular movements, but best known are the robot 'arms'. These can swivel at the 'waist' and have 'shoulder', 'elbow' and several 'wrist' joints. A 'hand' or gripper attached to the 'wrist' allows the robot to pick things up.

Robots need a 'brain' to remember their movements. This is generally based on a computer. To program movements into the robot, it has to be taught the positions of a number of places which it is to move between. An operator moves the robot to each position, perhaps to where a part will be picked up, using a special control box. These positions are stored in the computer memory. When

the computer program is run, the robot's computer looks up the positions and commands the robot to move to each in turn. The RobotArm program on pages 28 and 29 lets you have a go at driving a robot. As you will see, it is quite difficult, even in only two dimensions.

Many robots appear to move by magic. Humans have muscles to move. Instead of muscles, robots have actuators or motors to

To get to any point in space three basic axes of movement are possible: in and out; up and down; left and right. ▼

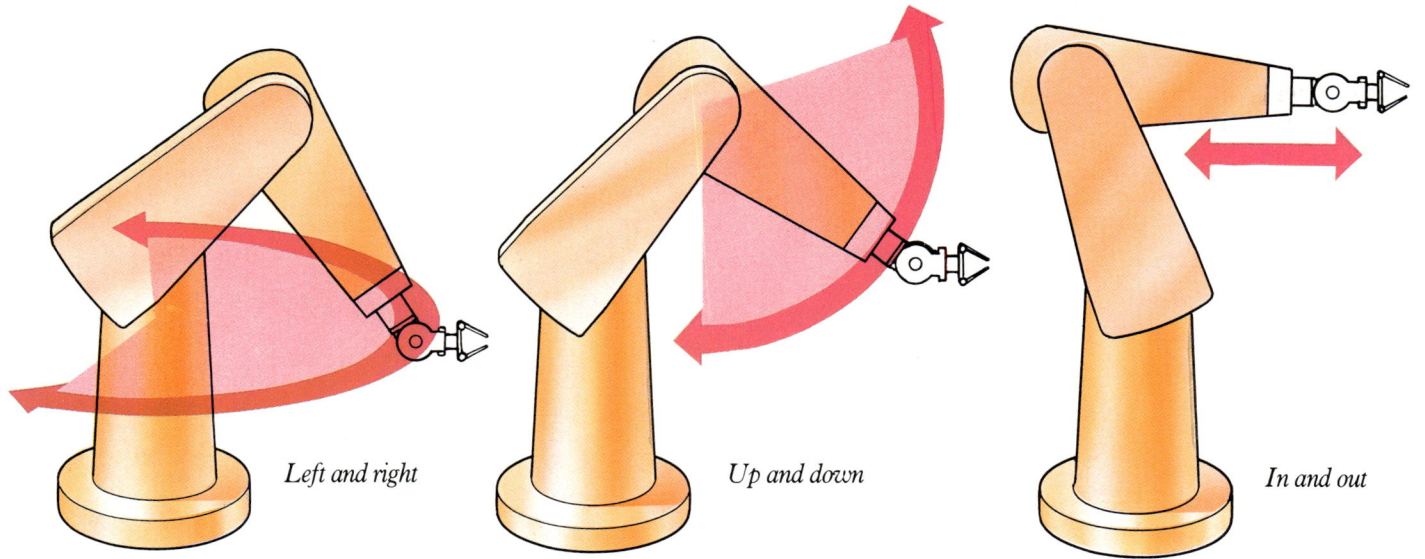

Left and right

Up and down

In and out

To get to any orientation in space, three rotational axes are possible: roll; pitch; yaw. ▼

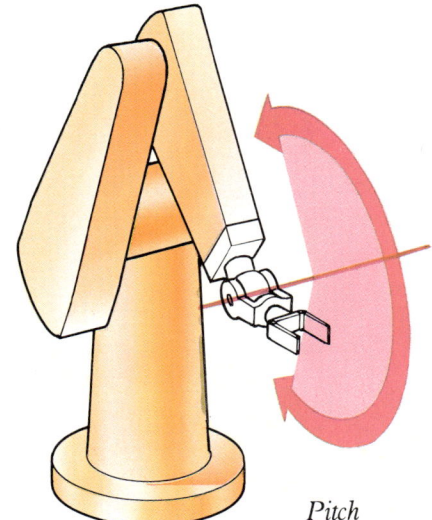

Pitch

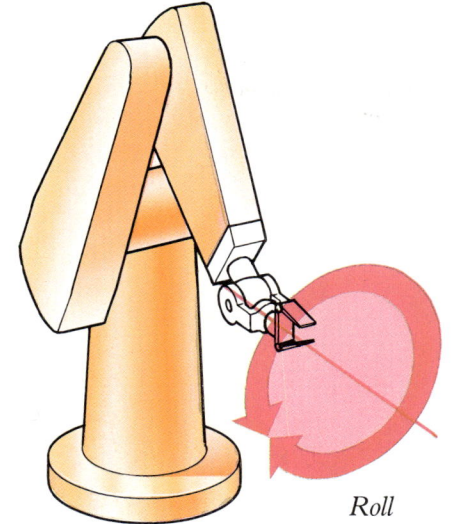

Roll

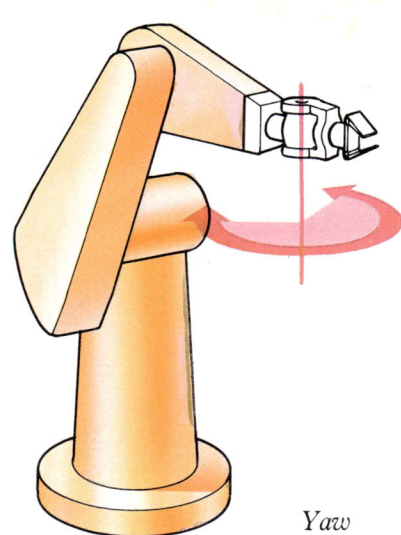

Yaw

power their movements. Each arm with a joint needs a motor to drive it. Often the main motors are mounted in the trunk of the robot and the drive is transferred to the joints. This is done with drive shafts or chains, just as the drive on your bicycle is transferred from the front cog, which you pedal, to the back wheel by the bicycle chain.

The motors are mounted in the trunk because they are very heavy. If they were mounted in the upper arm, the robot would have to lift the weight of the motors as well as any object held in the gripper.

The type of work a robot does best is determined by how its joints are arranged, and what 'muscles' or actuators it has. The actuators may be motors, which give rotary movements, or pistons, which give movement in straight lines.

Robots with rotating actuators have greater flexibility. They are used for spray painting and spot welding, as they are better at moving in confined spaces and following irregular paths. Robots with pistons are good at simple forward-backward movements, and are used for loading and unloading lathes and other machines. The pistons are forced in and out either by air pressure or by hydraulic fluid.

Program: ROBOTARM

In this program you control a robot. The robot has a gripping hand and an extendable arm. An apple appears on the screen and all you have to do is to use the robot to pick it up. Simple? Only to start with. There is a countdown – pick up the apple before the time runs out and you score points. But if you crush the apple, or run out of time, somebody else will pick up the apple and you get no apple and no points. The program has six skill levels. See how many points you can score. The robot arm is controlled by the cursor keys. Be warned! Once you start extending the arm you cannot bring it back. Make sure the gripper is in line with the apple before you extend the arm.

Type the program into the computer and make sure it runs properly. When typing the program in do not leave a space after the line number. This will make sure that the program fits into the available computer memory.

```
 10 MODE 1
 20 INPUT TAB(10,10)"Sound? Yes or No"
 30 Z=GET
 40 IF Z=89 v=-10 ELSE v=0:CLS
 50 DIM X(7):DIM Y(7):DIM OLDX(7):DIM OLDY(7)
 60 LEV=0:lev=50:Sc=0
 70 PROClevel
 80 PROCgraphics
 90 VDU 26:CLS:CLG
100 ext=FALSE:end=FALSE
110 VDU 23,1,0;0;0;0;
120 PROCsetup
130 VDU 23,1,0;0;0;0;
140 PROCstart
150 REPEAT
160   PROCsetold:PROCinput:PROCcoords
170   PROCunarm:PROCarm:PROCcheck
180   UNTIL ext=TRUE
190 IF end=TRUE GOTO 250
200 REPEAT
210   PROCextend:PROCcheck
220   UNTIL end=TRUE
230 *FX12,0
240 *FX21,0
250 CLS:PRINT"1 Another go     2 New player    3 S
top   Choose 1,2 or 3"
260 Z=GET:IF Z<49 OR Z>51 THEN 260
270 IF Z=49 GOTO 90 ELSE IF Z=50 RUN ELSE IF Z=5
1 THEN PROCend
280 END

290 DEF PROCpoint(dis,ANG)
300 x=Xmid+(dis*SIN(RAD(ANG)))
310 y=Ymid+(dis*COS(RAD(ANG)))
320 ENDPROC
330 DEF PROCarm
340 MOVE X(2),Y(2):MOVE X(3),Y(3):PLOT 85,X(4),Y
(4)
350 MOVE X(5),Y(5):MOVE X(6),Y(6):PLOT85,X(7),Y(
7)
360 ENDPROC
```

```
370 DEF PROCsetold
380 FOR count=1 TO 7
390   OLDX(count)=X(count)
400   OLDY(count)=Y(count)
410   NEXT
420 ENDPROC

430 DEF PROCunarm
440 MOVE OLDX(2),OLDY(2):MOVE OLDX(3),OLDY(3):PL
OT 87,OLDX(4),OLDY(4)
450 MOVE OLDX(5),OLDY(5):MOVE OLDX(6),OLDY(6):PL
OT 87,OLDX(7),OLDY(7)
460 ENDPROC

470 DEF PROCcoords
480 PROCpoint(rad+20,ang)
490 X(1)=x:Y(1)=y
500 PROCpoint(rad,ang+10)
510 X(2)=x:Y(2)=y
520 PROCpoint(rad+20,ang+20)
530 X(3)=x:Y(3)=y
540 PROCpoint(rad+60,ang+10)
550 X(4)=x:Y(4)=y
560 PROCpoint(rad,ang-10)
570 X(5)=x:Y(5)=y
580 PROCpoint(rad+20,ang-20)
590 X(6)=x:Y(6)=y
600 PROCpoint(rad+60,ang-10)
610 X(7)=x:Y(7)=y
620 ENDPROC

630 DEF PROCsetup
640 PROCmessage
650 VDU 24,0;96;1279;1023;
660 VDU 28,0,31,39,29
670 rand=RND(-TIME)
680 *FX4,1
690 *FX11,1
700 *FX12,1
710 GCOL 0,2
720 Xmid=640:Ymid=512:rad=100
730 FOR count=0 TO 72
740   ang=(2*PI)*(count/72)
750   X=(rad-5)*SIN(ang)
760   Y=(rad-5)*COS(ang)
770   MOVE Xmid,Ymid
780   PLOT 5,X+Xmid,Y+Ymid
790   NEXT
800 VDU 20,19,3,0,0,0,0
810 GCOL 0,1
820 PROCapple
830 GCOL 0,2
840 ang=0
850 PROCcoords
860 PROCarm
870 GCOL 0,2:COLOUR 2
880 ENDPROC

890 DEF PROCinput
900 IF INKEY(0)=-1 THEN GOTO 950
910 IF INKEY(0)=139 THEN LET ext=TRUE
920 IF INKEY(0)=136 THEN ang=ang-5
930 IF INKEY(0)=137 THEN ang=ang+5
940 *FX15,1
950 ENDPROC

960 DEF PROCextend
970 PROCunarm
980 PROCforearm
990 PROCarm
1000 PROCextendcentre
1010 PROCsetold
1020 PROCcoords
1030 ENDPROC
```

```
1040 DEF PROCextendcentre
1050 Xmid=Xmid+(10*SIN(RAD(ang)))
1060 Ymid=Ymid+(10*COS(RAD(ang)))
1070 ENDPROC
1080 DEF PROCforearm
1090 MOVE OLDX(2),OLDY(2):DRAW X(5),Y(5)
1100 ENDPROC


1110 DEF PROCapple
1120 apang=5*RND(9*LEV)
1130 IF RND(2)>1 THEN apang=apang-(2*apang)
1140 LOCAL rad
1150  rad=10*RND(45)
1160 Xap=Xmid+(rad*SIN(RAD(apang)))
1170 Yap=Ymid+(rad*COS(RAD(apang)))
1180 IF Xap>400 AND Xap<900 AND Yap>300 AND Yap<7
00 THEN GOTO 1110
1190 IF POINT(Xap,Yap)=-1THEN GOTO 1110
1200 VDU 5
1210 MOVE Xap-16,Yap+16
1220 VDU 240,4
1230 countdown=((3*(rad/100)/(Yap/100))+lev+5)DIV
1
1240 ENDPROC


1250 DEF PROCcheck
1260 PROCtime
1270 A$="You´ve crushed the apple."
1280 IF POINT(Xap,Yap)=2 THEN PROCendbad
1290 IF Y(1)-Yap<5 AND Y(1)-Yap>-5 AND X(1)-Xap<5
AND X(1)-Xap>-5 THEN PROCendgood
1300 ENDPROC


1310 DEF PROCendgood
1320 CLS:PRINT"Got it!";
1330 Sc=Sc+((countdown-time)*LEV)
1340 PRINT TAB(20,0)"Score ";(countdown-time)*LEV
1350 PROClevel:PROCsound
1360 end=TRUE
1370 ENDPROC


1380 DEF PROCstart
1390 start=TIME
1400 PROCtime
1410 ENDPROC


1420 DEF PROCtime
1430 time=(TIME-start)DIV 100
1440 PRINT TAB(0,0)"SECONDS ";countdown-time" "
1450 PRINT TAB(20,0)"Skill level ";LEV
1460 PRINT TAB(20,1)"Total score ";Sc
1470 A$="Sorry...time´s up."
1480 IF countdown-time=0 PROCendbad
1490 ENDPROC


1500 DEF PROCendbad
1510 CLS:VDU 7:PRINT TAB(0,0)A$
1520 PROCtruck
1530 ext=TRUE:end=TRUE
1540 ENDPROC

1550 DEF PROCmessage
1560 VDU 19,3,2,0,0,0
1570 COLOUR 3
1580 PRINT TAB(15,2)"ROBOT  ARM"´
1590 PRINT TAB(13,4)CHR$241;" =turn left"
1600 PRINT TAB(13,6)CHR$242;" =turn right"
1610 PRINT TAB(13,8)CHR$243;" =extend arm"
1620 ENDPROC


1630 DEF PROClevel
1640 LEV=LEV+1:lev=lev-5
1650 ENDPROC


1660 DEF PROCtruck
1670 COLOUR 1
1680 LOCAL count
1690 CLG:VDU 28,0,31,39,0
1700 trux=(Xap/32)DIV 1
1710 truy=32-(Yap/32)DIV 1
1720 PRINT TAB(trux,truy)CHR$240
1730 C$=" "+CHR$244+CHR$245+CHR$246+" "
1740 B$=" "+CHR$247+CHR$248+CHR$249+" "
1750 FOR count=1 TO trux-4
1760    PRINT TAB(count,truy-1)C$
1770    PRINT TAB(count,truy)B$
1780    FOR wt=1 TO 100:NEXT wt
1790    NEXT count
1800 B$=" "+CHR$247+CHR$248+CHR$249+CHR$240+" "
1810 FOR count=trux-4 TO 0 STEP -1
1820    PRINT TAB(count,truy-1)C$
1830    PRINT TAB(count,truy)B$
1840    FOR wt=1 TO 100:NEXT wt
1850    NEXT count
1860 VDU 28,0,31,39,29
1870 VDU 24,0;96;1279;1023;
1880 COLOUR 2:CLG
1890 ENDPROC


1900 DEF PROCgraphics
1910 REM apple
1920 VDU 23,240,0,24,16,126,255,239,103,118
1930 REM arrows
1940 VDU 23,241,16,32,64,255,64,32,16,0
1950 VDU 23,242,8,4,3,255,2,4,8,0
1960 VDU 23,243,16,56,84,146,16,16,16,16
1970 REM truck
1980 VDU 23,244,0,6,79,70,79,84,127,127
1990 VDU 23,245,0,16,56,80,144,30,254,255
2000 VDU 23,246,0,128,128,128,128,128,128
2010 VDU 23,247,127,127,3,49,120,120,48,0
2020 VDU 23,248,255,255,193,153,60,60,24,0
2030 VDU 23,249,128,128,128,128,128,252,0,0
2040 ENDPROC


2050 DEF PROCsound
2060 x=0
2070 FOR y=1 TO 10
2080    SOUND 1,v,x+53,2:SOUND 1,v,x+69,2
2090    SOUND 1,v,x+81,2:SOUND 1,v,x+101,2
2100    SOUND 1,v,x+81,2:SOUND 1,v,x+69,2
2110    x=x+4
2120    NEXT
2130 ENDPROC


2140 DEF PROCend
2150 *FX21,0
2160 *FX4,0
2170 VDU 26
2180 CLS:PRINT TAB(15,10)"Goodbye"
2190 ENDPROC
```

Entertaining robots

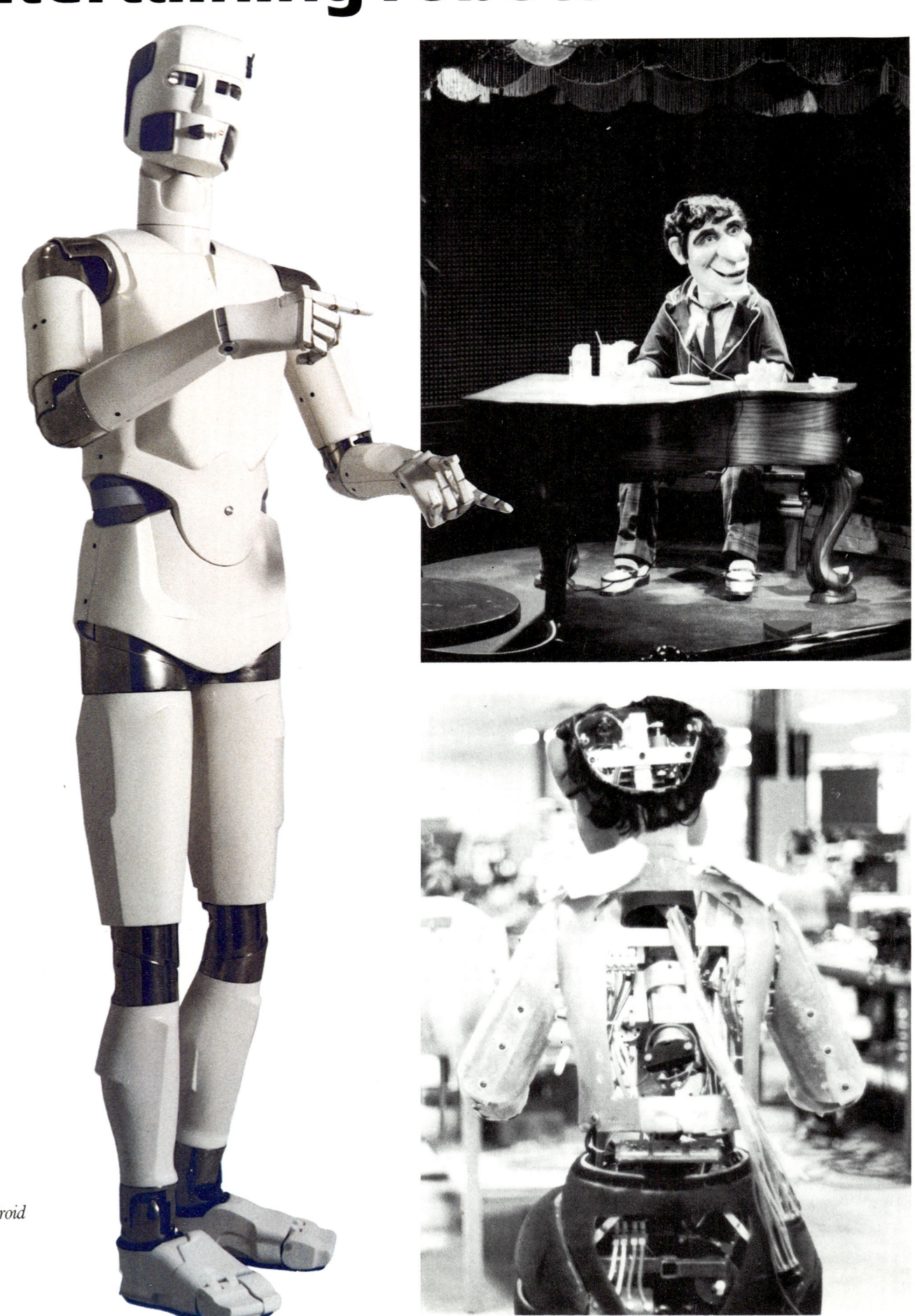

MacAndroid

Although most robots work hard in factories, a few have a more glamorous occupation. Following in the tradition of ancient automata, some of today's robots are made to delight and entertain. Walt Disney knew the attraction of robots and filled his fantasy lands with them, from elephants with flapping ears to a talking President Lincoln. Many of these moving figures and animals cannot easily be reprogrammed to change the movements they make, and so are not really robots. The elephants at Disneyland have

◄ *MacAndroid (far left) is a robotic film star. He is computer controlled, but his joints are driven by compressed air.*

◄ *Sammy Sands is a popular robotic entertainer in the United States. It can move, talk and sing to the audience. The rear view of Sammy Sands shows the pneumatic cylinders and electronic valves that control the machine.*

▲ *The rear view of the scribe shows the clockwork mechanisms which enabled movement without the power of electricity.*

been flapping their ears for years, but, although their ears may be wearing out, they can't be re-programmed to wave their trunks instead.

Robots are also used for promotion and advertising. Anything that attracts a crowd can be used to sell products, and robots certainly attract crowds. In the United States, robots are even used to sell pizza. The world's biggest robot rat is Chuck E Cheese, the two metre computer controlled mascot of a chain of pizza restaurants. However, many of the robots used to promote products are radio controlled. A hidden operator drives the robot using a control box. The instructions from the box are turned into radio waves, and transmitted to the robot.

▲ *This clockwork scribe delighted audiences in the eighteenth century, who marvelled at his skill and penmanship.*

Many of the automata from the eighteenth century had quite a repertoire. There was the clockwork pianist with a fantastically intricate mechanism which allowed her to play eighteen different tunes, and a flute player which could play twelve tunes. Our modern equivalents are limited only by what is recorded on their tape players, but to play eighteen tunes without the aid of electricity seems more of an achievement. The family of Pierre Jacquet-Droz (1721–1790) made many fabulous toys, including a sheep that bleated in a lifelike manner. Perhaps their most famous creation was the 'Young Writer' or Scribe, pictured here. The clockwork mechanism inside him can be adjusted to write different words.

Robots in space

The Soviet moon 'jeep' from Lunokhod 2 on the moon in 1973.

▲ *The Soviet moon 'jeep' from Lunokhod 2 on the moon in 1973.*

Space is airless, weightless, and very cold, a harsh environment for living things. Ideally space exploration should be carried out by humans, as we can be far more selective in what we examine than any robot. Most robot satellites transmit vast amounts of information back to Earth, but only a fraction of it is useful. However it is difficult to support human life in space for extended periods. A round trip to Mars would take about eighteen months, during which time a human crew would have to be fed and supplied with oxygen. Also, being weightless for this length of time may damage the human body. Robot explorers

▲ *This artist's impression looks ahead to the future construction in space of solar powered satellites. The six automated beam builders (in white) would be used to construct beams for the main structure (in orange).*

have been used as they need less protection against the harsh environment of space, and don't mind a one way trip.

Perhaps the first robot explorer was the Soviet Lunokhod 1, sent to the moon in 1970. It roamed the lunar surface for eleven months, sending back data.

Lunokhod 1 and 2 were followed by Viking 1 and 2, two of the most sophisticated pilotless spacecraft ever built. Their mission was to explore the surface of Mars. To do this, one section of the spacecraft, the Lander, was to soft land on the

◀ *Viking 1 landed on Mars on July 20 1976. Its television cameras sent pictures of the surface of Mars back to Earth. In the photograph you can see an arm carrying meteorological instruments for measuring the weather on Mars. On the right are some trenches dug by its soil sampling arm.*

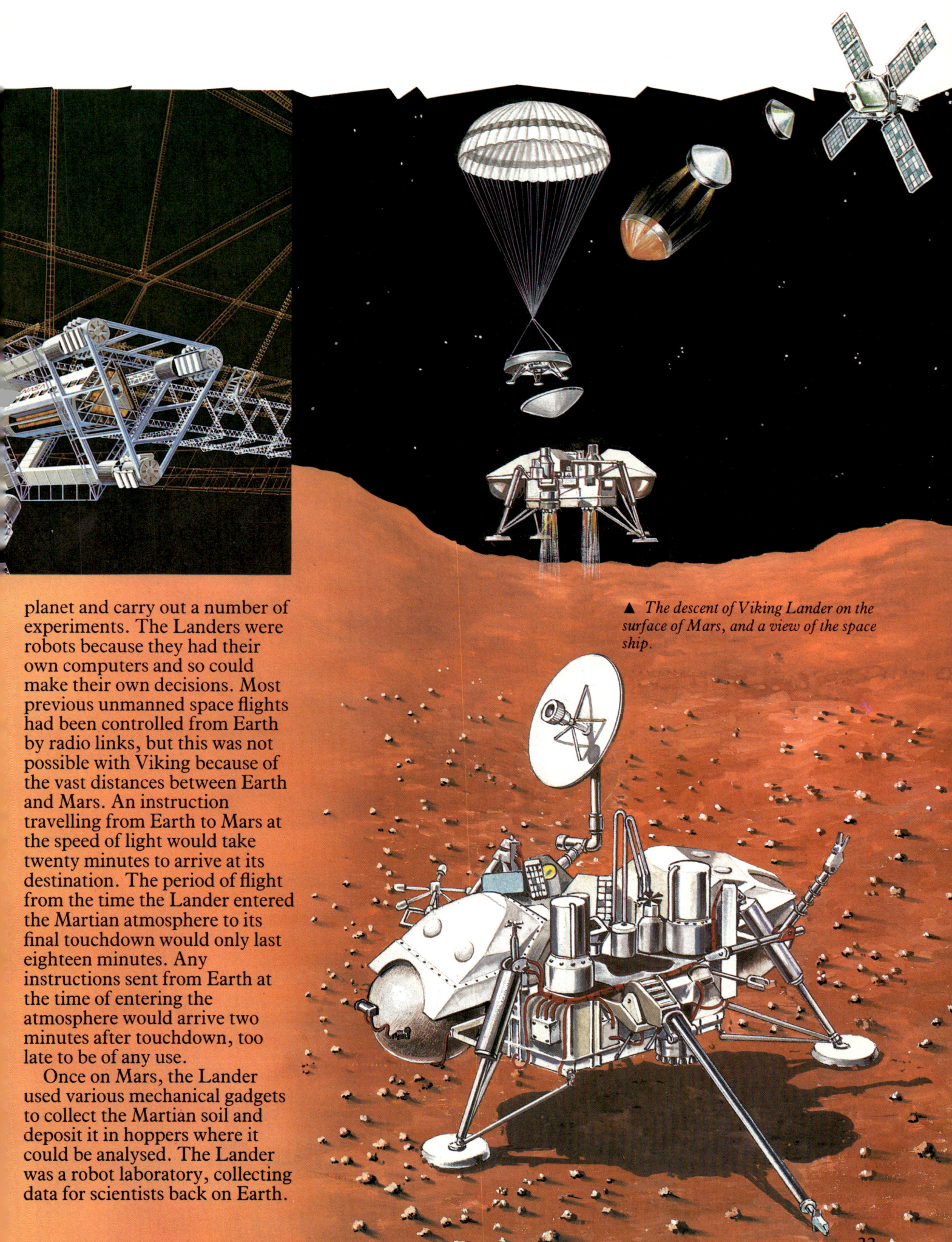

planet and carry out a number of experiments. The Landers were robots because they had their own computers and so could make their own decisions. Most previous unmanned space flights had been controlled from Earth by radio links, but this was not possible with Viking because of the vast distances between Earth and Mars. An instruction travelling from Earth to Mars at the speed of light would take twenty minutes to arrive at its destination. The period of flight from the time the Lander entered the Martian atmosphere to its final touchdown would only last eighteen minutes. Any instructions sent from Earth at the time of entering the atmosphere would arrive two minutes after touchdown, too late to be of any use.

Once on Mars, the Lander used various mechanical gadgets to collect the Martian soil and deposit it in hoppers where it could be analysed. The Lander was a robot laboratory, collecting data for scientists back on Earth.

▲ *The descent of Viking Lander on the surface of Mars, and a view of the space ship.*

33

The home as a robot

Since people built their first homes, they have tried to make them more comfortable. The first shelters just kept out the rain, but as each new technology appeared, it was adapted to improve the quality of home life. Better building materials, running water, electric light and central heating all contribute to the comfort of a modern home. The computer is another development which will be integrated into home design, bringing better control over our home environment.

Our homes are like life-support systems, built to keep us warm and dry, healthy and well fed. Nowadays we also expect the home to provide us with entertainment (by television), and communication (by telephone). A computer can improve our control over all these functions, reducing wastage of energy and human time.

The home of the future is unlikely to be staffed by domestic robots. Each house might have a robot 'butler' whose duties would be to fetch and carry around the house, but the robot butler and all other machines in the house would be under the control of one central computer. This computer would have an 'eye' and an 'ear' in every room, to give it sensory feedback from its environment. Its capabilities might range from adjusting the room temperature to keeping watch for burglars.

The central computer would be connected to a network of other computers through which it could order the weekly shopping from a supermarket computer, and arrange communication links between the family and the outside world.

◄ *An artist's impression of the robotic home of the future features a central computer shaft, which activates and controls the environment.*

1 Electric track in the road may regulate traffic, and guide automated delivery vans.

2 Television cameras and robots may control security for the house.

3 Infra-red beams and card keys may be used to open door locks.

4 Automatic delivery port serves every floor.

5 Central core computer may control all the robotic features of the house.

Artificial intelligence

People who work with computers are trying to get machines to do things that we call 'intelligent'. Today's robots behave pretty stupidly, and are stumped by simple problems, like how to put an egg into an eggbox when the lid is shut. We solve problems like this by making plans, thinking out the possible ways round a problem, and deciding which is best. Most robots don't 'know' enough about how boxes work, and would probably try to push the egg through the lid. Robots have been programmed to make their own plans, but only for simple problems like stacking building bricks.

Our brains are very good at memorising odd bits of information in a jumbled way, and later remembering bits of it which might help to solve a problem. Computers have to store data in a very structured, rigid way, and this can make it difficult to get at the right information to solve a problem.

We can draw out a plan in a 'tree diagram'; this looks like an upside down tree, with the tree's branches showing the possible choices. Computers often store their plans in a 'tree', and search up and down the branches to find the best route to a problem's solution. A computer could play chess by looking down a tree of all possible moves in a game, but it would take longer than the life of our sun to play this way, because of the enormous number of possible moves. Computers can now play expert chess, because like us, they speed up their play by only considering the most interesting moves.

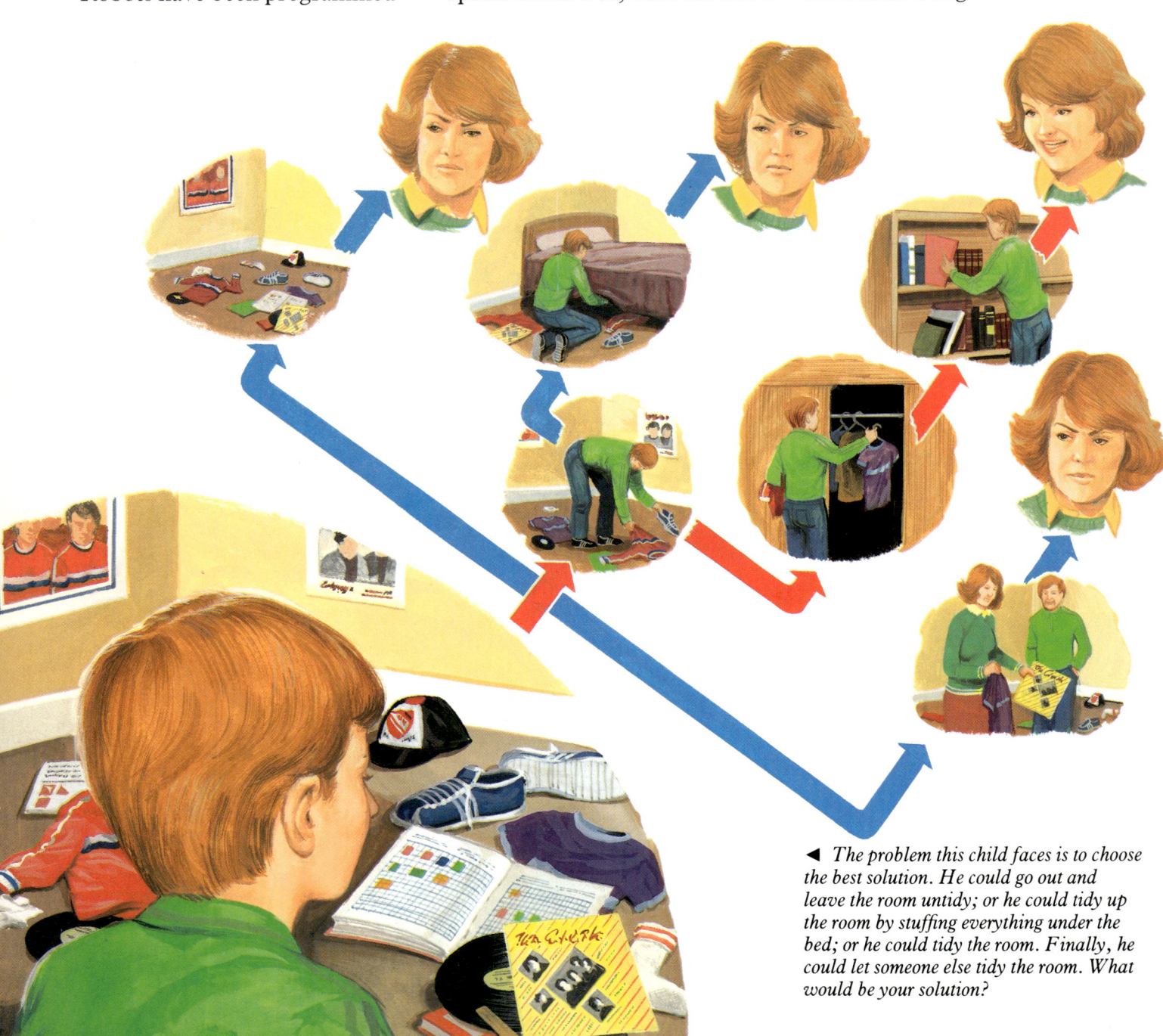

◄ *The problem this child faces is to choose the best solution. He could go out and leave the room untidy; or he could tidy up the room by stuffing everything under the bed; or he could tidy the room. Finally, he could let someone else tidy the room. What would be your solution?*

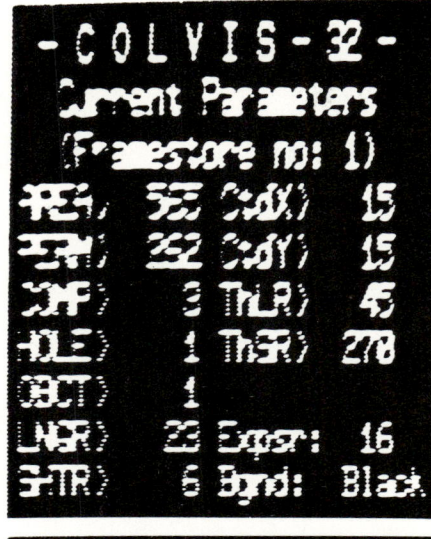

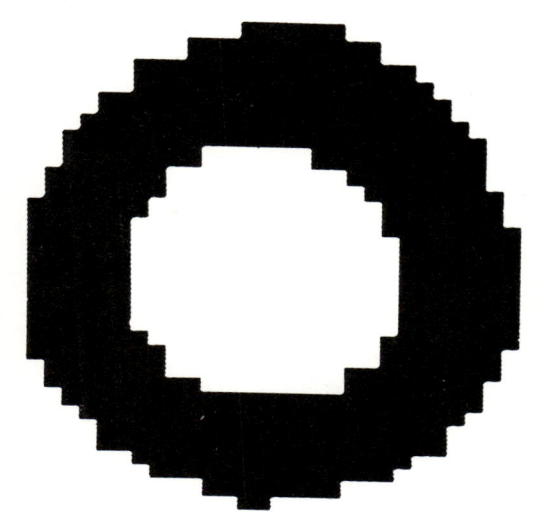

▲ *A computer has great difficulty in 'seeing' objects. This VDU screen shows a computer's view of a perfect circle.*

This optical illusion demonstrates how the human eye can be deceived by what it sees. ▶

We can very easily recognise simple shapes, but just take a look at the measurements and calculations a robot has to make before it can recognise a circle. It takes several seconds to do this.

Our brains have evolved special techniques for recognising shapes quickly. However, sometimes our brains can be deceived. Is there a triangle in the picture above, or is it just three Pacmen? Our mechanism for recognising objects is very complex, and in this case our brain can interpret the picture either way.

One of the problems with trying to make robots more intelligent is the long time computers take to recognise patterns and make plans. We can recognise things quickly because different sections of our brain are thinking about different features of the picture at the same time. While one bit of the brain is looking at the edges of the shape, another is looking at the colour, and another at the texture. All these bits of the brain are working together in parallel. In contrast, today's computers have to queue up all their measurements and calculations to be done one after another in their single 'central processor'.

Computers are now being designed that will have teams of 'parallel processors' working together on a problem. These computers, known as the 'Fifth Generation', will be very fast, and will help people make more intelligent robots.

Expert robots

We rely on the knowledge of experts to solve many of our problems, from what to do when we fall ill, to why our car won't go. An expert is someone who has spent a lot of time studying a subject, and has reinforced this study with years of practical experience. We say the expert 'knows' a lot more about the subject than most of us.

Many poor countries need more experts to help them solve their problems with health and food. In parts of Africa for example, villages are without health care and patients may have to walk for days to visit a doctor. Human expertise is expensive as it is only gained after many years of study, training and experience. In the future 'computer doctors' should be available cheaply, so that villages in Africa and elsewhere that cannot afford to support a human doctor can still have expert medical advice.

Artificial intelligence researchers are beginning to produce expert computer programs. These programs use facts and rules to give them 'knowledge' about a problem. Similarly, armed with facts like 'brown toast is tasty' and 'black toast is nasty', and rules like 'if the toast turns black switch off the grill', you might become an expert at making toast.

At the moment, expert programs only work well with limited problems. An expert toaster is possible, but a computer cook would need hundreds of rules and facts. Attempts at producing more general 'experts on everything' have not been very successful. Eventually expert robots, full of knowledge about medicine and growing food, will work tirelessly to feed and cure us. We might even vote for an expert computer government!

International industrial enterprises may produce mobile clinics and other goods in robot controlled factories.

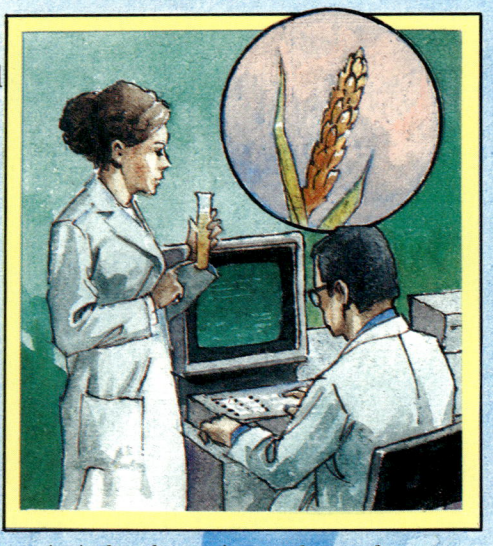

Agricultural expertise may be stored on computers to help farmers improve their crops. Robots may control the irrigation and harvesting of locally grown crops.

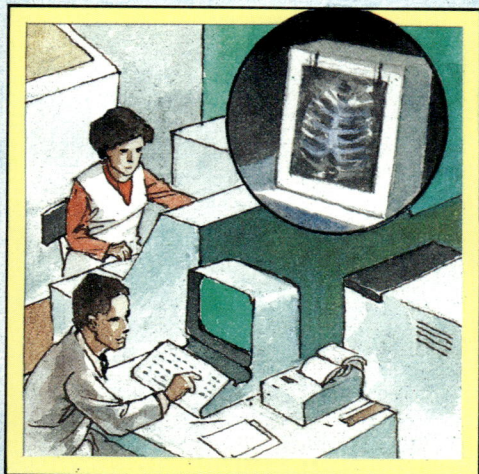

Medical knowledge such as the results of a radiographic analysis may be available through the use of mobile computer clinics. Local people may be able to describe medical symptoms to the computer, which will then recommend the correct treatment.

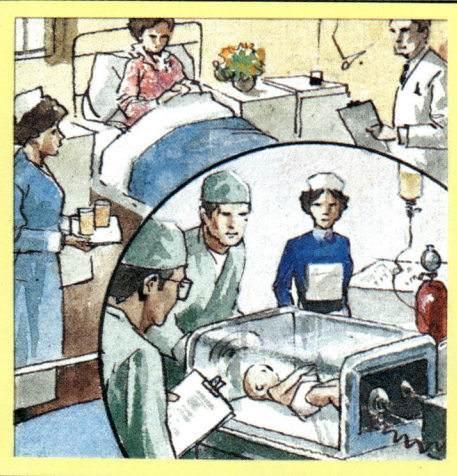

The health of babies and young children may be improved through the availability of computer assisted information. Correct nutrition and care may ensure a healthier population.

Education and all of human knowledge may be available to children in school through computer links and robot teachers in the classroom.

Computers and robots will be used increasingly in the future to provide communications, agriculture, medicine, health education and industry.

This program shows how a robot can learn about its surroundings. The game is set in a room which is shown on the screen as a grid of squares. The robot starts at the top left hand corner and is trying to cross the room to the bottom right hand corner. You are making problems for the robot by building a maze of obstacles across the room. The robot must then find a new route through the room.

The robot solves the problem in two stages. First it moves through the room exploring the maze and building up a picture of the room in its memory. In the second stage the robot shows you what it has learned about its new surroundings.

The program starts by showing you a list of options. These are:
1. Demonstration
This option sets an obstacle and shows how the robot learns about its new surroundings.
2. Set obstacles
Lets you place obstacles in the room.
3. Clear obstacles
Clears all the obstacles out of the room.
4. Display the robot's memory
Shows you how the robot sees the room by printing out the contents of its memory. Look inside a robot's brain?

Type the program into the computer and debug it so that it runs properly. Save the program on cassette.

```
  10 MODE 5
  20 REM **THE LEARNING ROBOT**
  30 PROCinitialise
  40 PROCmenu
  50 COLOUR 3
  60 *FX4,0
  70 CLS:PRINT TAB(5,15)"Goodbye"
  80 END

  90 DEF PROCinitialise
 100  DIM move(300,2):DIM priority
(4,2)
 110 DIM memory(20,20):DIM grid$(2
0)
```

```
 120 move=0
 130 VDU 23,1,0;0;0;0;

 140 VDU 23,240,255,129,129,129,12
9,129,129,255
 150 VDU 23,241,110,223,183,111,22
3,251,247,110
 160 VDU 23,242,60,90,90,126,60,12
4,231,0
 170 VDU 19,2,2,0,0,0
 180 LOCAL count
 190 FOR count=1 TO 4
 200    READ priority(count,1)
 210    READ priority(count,2)
 220    NEXT count
 230 DATA 0,1,1,0,0,-1,-1,0
 240 PROCsetgrid

 250 DEF PROCmenu
 260 quit=FALSE
 270 REPEAT
 280    CLS
 290    COLOUR 1
 300    PRINT TAB(1,5)"THE LEARNING
ROBOT"
 310        COLOUR 3
 320    PRINT TAB(0,9)"1 Demonstrat
ion"
 330    PRINT TAB(0,11)"2 Set obsta
cles"
 340    PRINT TAB(0,13)"3 Clear obs
tacles"
 350    PRINT TAB(0,15)"4 Display r
obot´s"
 360    PRINT TAB(2,17)"memory"
 370    PRINT TAB(0,19)"5 Stop the
game"
 380    COLOUR 1
 390    PRINT TAB(1,25)"Choose from
1 to 5"
 400    Z=GET
 410    IF Z=49 THEN PROCdemo ELSE
IF Z=50 THEN PROCobstacles ELSE  IF
 Z=51 THEN PROCclearall ELSE IF Z=5
2 THEN PROCmemory
 420    UNTIL Z=53
 430 ENDPROC

 440 DEF PROCdemo
 450 grid$(4)=STRING$(10,CHR$240)+
STRING$(4,CHR$241)+STRING$(6,CHR$24
0)
```

```
 460 grid$(6)=STRING$(7,CHR$240)+S
TRING$(7,CHR$241)+STRING$(6,CHR$240
)
 470 grid$(8)=STRING$(4,CHR$240)+S
TRING$(10,CHR$241)+STRING$(6,CHR$24
0)
 480 grid$(10)=STRING$(14,CHR$241)
+STRING$(6,CHR$240)
 490 grid$(5)=STRING$(13,CHR$240)+
STRING$(1,CHR$241)+STRING$(6,CHR$24
0)
 500 grid$(7)=grid$(5):grid$(9)=gr
id$(5)
 510 CLS
 520 PROCfirstrun
 530 ENDPROC


 540 DEF PROCobstacles
 550 LOCAL quit:quit=FALSE
 560 X=0:Y=0:Xnew=0:Ynew=0
 570 *FX4,1
 580 CLS:PROCgrid
 590 COLOUR 1
 600 PRINT TAB(X,Y+4)"*"
 610 COLOUR 3
 620 PRINT TAB(0,25)"Use arrow key
s to"
 630 PRINT"move around the room"
 640 Z=INKEY(500)
 650 PRINT TAB(0,25)"Space bar-set
 blocks"
 660 PRINT"R-remove blocks        "
 670 PRINT"F-to finish"
 680 A$=CHR$240
 690 REPEAT
 700    Z=GET
 710    IF Z>135 AND Z<140 THEN PRO
Cmove ELSE IF Z=32 THEN PROCblock(2
41) ELSE IF Z=82 OR Z=114 THEN PROC
block(240)
 720    IF Z=70 THEN quit=TRUE
 730    UNTIL quit=TRUE
 740 CLS
 750 PROCfirstrun
 760 ENDPROC


 770 DEF PROCmemory
 780 CLS
 790 FOR count=1 TO 20
 800    FOR number=1 TO 20
 810       IF memory(number,count)=1
 THEN LET A$=CHR$241 ELSE A$=CHR$24
0
 820       PRINT TAB(number-1,count+
3);A$
 830       NEXT number
 840    NEXT count
 850 COLOUR2
 860    FOR print=1 TO move
 870     PRINT TAB(move(print,1),mov
e(print,2)+4)CHR$242
 880     NEXTprint
 890 PRINT TAB(5,30)"Press any key
"
 900 Z=GET
 910 ENDPROC


 920 DEF PROCgrid
 930 CLS
 940 VDU 10,10,10,10
 950 LOCAL count:COLOUR 2
 960 FOR count=1 TO 20
 970    PRINT grid$(count);
 980    NEXT count
 990 ENDPROC


1000 DEF PROCmove
1010 IF Z=137 THEN LET Xnew=X+1
1020 IF Z=136 THEN LET Xnew=X-1
1030 IF Z=139 THEN LET Ynew=Y-1
1040 IF Z=138 THEN LET Ynew=Y+1
1050 IF Xnew<0 OR Xnew=20 THEN Xne
w=X
1060 IF Ynew<0 OR Ynew=20THEN Ynew
=Y
1070 COLOUR2
1080 PRINT TAB(X,Y+4)MID$(grid$(Y+
1),X+1,1)
1090 COLOUR1
1100 PRINT TAB(Xnew,Ynew+4)"*"
1110 X=Xnew:Y=Ynew
1120 COLOUR 2:Z=0
1130 ENDPROC


1140 DEF PROCblock(char)
1150 PRINT TAB(X,Y+4)CHR$char
1160 grid$(Y+1)=LEFT$(grid$(Y+1),X
)+CHR$char+MID$(grid$(Y+1),X+2,20)
1170 ENDPROC
```

```
1180 DEF PROCfirstrun                 1610 DEF PROCmakemove
1190 PROCgrid:PROCclear               1620 PRINT TAB(X,Y+4)CHR$240
1200 X=0:Y=0:move=0                   1630 memory(Xnew+1,Ynew+1)=1
1210 arrival=FALSE                    1640 COLOUR 3
1220 check=1                          1650 PRINT TAB(Xnew,Ynew+4)CHR$242
1230 PROCescape                       1660 COLOUR 2
1240 IF escape=TRUE THEN GOTO 1680    1670 X=Xnew:Y=Ynew
1250 IF check>4 THEN LET check=1:P    1680 ENDPROC
ROCbackup
1260 Xnew=X+priority(check,1)
1270 Ynew=Y+priority(check,2)
1280 IF Xnew<0 OR Xnew>19 THEN che
ck=check+1:GOTO 1230
1290 IF Ynew<0 OR Ynew>19 THEN che    1690 DEF PROCcheckarrival
ck=check+1:GOTO 1230                  1700 IF X=19 AND Y=19 THEN arrival
1300 IF MID$(grid$(Ynew+1),Xnew+1,   =TRUE
1)=CHR$241 THEN LET check=check+1:m    1710 ENDPROC
emory(Xnew+1,Ynew+1)=1:GOTO 1230
1310 IF memory(Xnew+1,Ynew+1)=1 TH
EN LET check=check+1:GOTO 1230
1320 count=0                          1720 DEF PROCturnback
1330 move=move+1                      1730 FOR change=count TO move
1340 REPEAT                           1740    LET memory(move(change,1),m
1350    count=count+1                 ove(change,2))=1
1360    IF move(count,1)=Xnew AND m   1750    NEXT change
ove(count,2)=Ynew THEN PROCturnback   1760 LET move=count
1370    UNTIL count=move              1770 ENDPROC
1380 move(count,1)=Xnew
1390 move(count,2)=Ynew
1400 PROCmakemove
1410 PROCcheckarrival
1420 IF arrival=FALSE GOTO 1220       1780 DEF PROCsecondrun
1430 PROCsecondrun                    1790 COLOUR3
1440 ENDPROC                          1800   PRINT TAB(0,25)"Press any ke
                                      y for"´
                                      1810 PRINT"the second run        "
                                      1820 COLOUR2
1450 DEF PROCbackup                   1830 Z=GET
1460 LOCAL count                      1840 X=0:Y=0:Xnew=0:Ynew=0
1470 count=move-1                     1850 count=0:arrival=FALSE
1480   IF move<1 OR count<1 THEN PR   1860 REPEAT
OCstuck:GOTO 1620                     1870    count=count+1
1490 Xnew=move(count,1)               1880    Xnew=move(count,1)
1500 Ynew=move(count,2)               1890    Ynew=move(count,2)
1510 PROCmakemove                     1900    PROCmakemove
1520 n=1                              1910    FOR pause=1 TO 200:NEXT pau
1530 b=(Xnew+priority(n,1))+1:IF b   se
<1 OR b>20THEN 1580                   1920    PROCcheckarrival
1540 c=(Ynew+priority(n,2))+1:IF c   1930    UNTIL arrival=TRUE
<1 OR c>20THEN 1580                   1940 COLOUR3
1550 a=memory(b,c)                    1950    PRINT TAB(0,25)"Would you l
1560 b$=MID$((grid$(c)),b,1)          ike to"´
1570 IF a=0 AND b$=CHR$240 THEN mo    1960 PRINT"see that again? Y/N"
ve=count:GOTO 1620                    1970 COLOUR2
1580 n=n+1:IF n<5 GOTO 1530           1980 Z=GET
1590 count=count-1:GOTO 1480          1990 IF Z=89 THEN GOTO 1840
1600 ENDPROC                          2000 ENDPROC
```

```
2010 DEF PROCclear
2020 FOR clear=1 TO 20
2030    memory(clear,1)=0
2040    FOR number=1 TO 20
2050      memory(clear,number)=0
2060      NEXT number
2070    NEXT clear
2080 FOR clear=1 TO 300
2090    move(clear,1)=0:move(clear,
2)=0
2100    NEXTclear
2110 ENDPROC

2120 DEF PROCescape
2130 COLOUR3
2140 PRINT TAB(0,25)"Stop with any
key"
2150 COLOUR2
2160 escape=FALSE
2170 IF INKEY(0)<>-1 THEN escape=T
RUE
2180 ENDPROC
```

```
2190 DEF PROCsetgrid
2200    FOR count=1 TO 20
2210      LET grid$(count)=STRING$(20
CHR$240)
2220      NEXTcount
2230 ENDPROC


2240 DEF PROCclearall
2250 CLS:PRINT TAB(5,15)"Clearing"
2260 PROCclear
2270 PROCsetgrid
2280 ENDPROC



2290 DEF PROCstuck
2300 COLOUR1
2310   PRINT TAB(0,27)"This maze ha
s no"
2320 PRINT"way out!"
2330 ENDPROC
```

Hint

*Try designing your maze on a piece of squared paper before
setting a problem for the robot. This will make it easier for you to
set complicated mazes for the robot. The room is 20 squares wide
by 20 squares deep. You could try the maze shown below.
Experiment by adding more walls to the maze.*

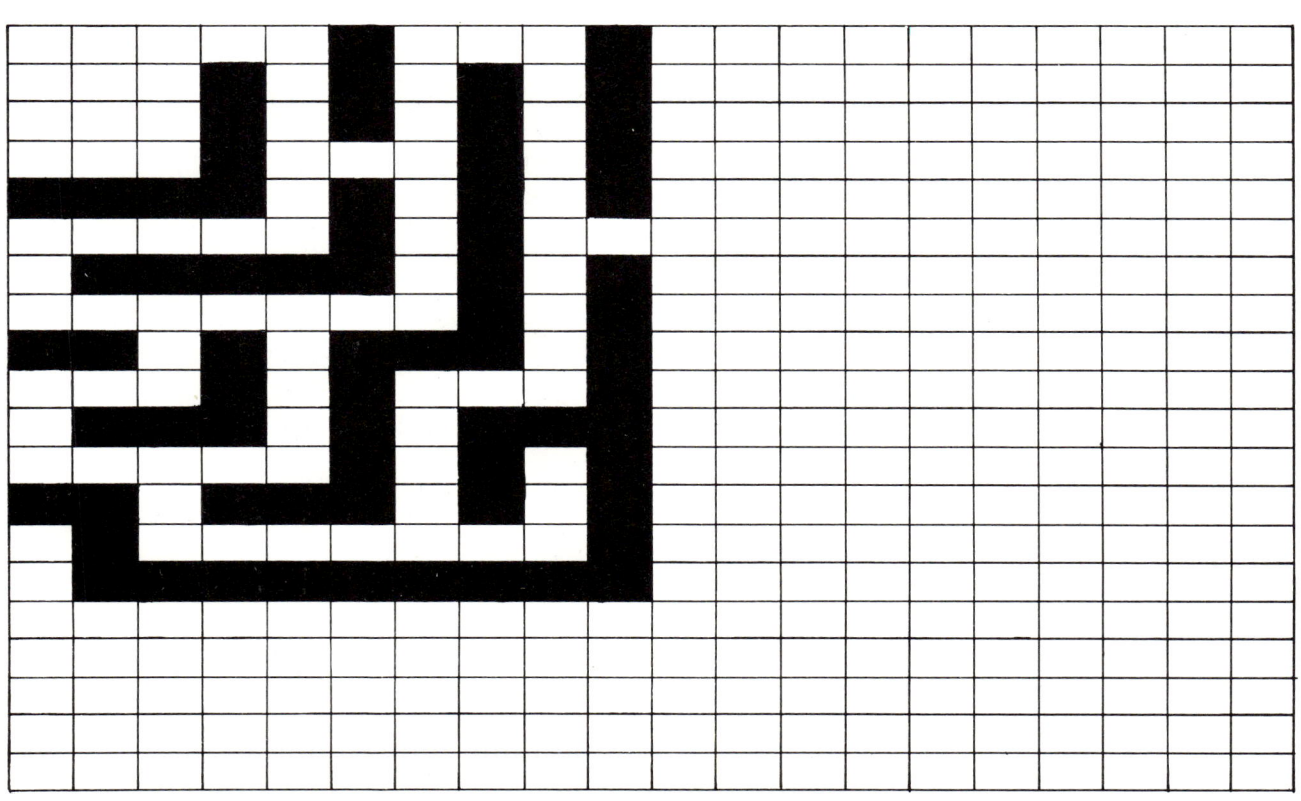

Robot words

Accuracy The ability of a robot to move to a point defined by the operator.

Actuator A device which enables robots to move. *Motors* and *pistons* are both different types of actuator.

Alpha-numeric display An electronic display that can display numbers and letters.

Array A series of similar objects arranged together eg an array of *photo-electric cells*.

Artificial intelligence The process used by a machine to work out a course of action or behave in a manner that we would call intelligent.

Automata Machines, often mechanical figures, which simulate the actions of living beings and appear to move spontaneously, but in which the source of power is hidden.

Bar code A pattern of stripes which carries information about a product. The pattern is read by a light pen or *laser* beam.

Carburettor A device in a car engine which converts liquid petrol into vapour.

Force sensor A sensor which tells a robot how hard it is forcing or pushing down on a surface, for example it can tell how much force the robot is having to exert to push a peg into a hole.

Ignition The firing of the explosive mixture of petrol and air in the cylinder of a car engine. Computer controlled ignition regulates more efficiently the intervals of time at which the mixture is ignited.

Infra-red link A means of sending information from one point to another using infra-red radiation, for example the remote control of a television.

Laser A device that produces an intense, highly concentrated beam of light.

Learnt parameters Measurements stored in a computer memory and used when it attempts to identify objects.

Optical illusion A picture or illustration which when viewed can be interpreted by the brain in two different ways.

Photo-electric cell A tiny piece of material which reacts to the amount of light falling on it, and allows electricity to flow through it in proportion to the amount of light available.

Piston A robot *actuator* used for in-out movements, driven by hydraulic fluid or air pressure.

Pixel The small squares into which a computer screen is divided for graphics.

Precision The ability of a robot to go back to the same place time after time. Also known as *repeatability*.

Reflex An involuntary response to a stimulus.

Repeatability see *Precision*.

Sensor A device which can turn information from the outside world into electrical signals.

Servo amplifier A device which enlarges or amplifies small signals in a servo system into signals which drive servo motors.

Servo mechanism An automatic control device by which you can put in a demand signal and a servo motor will follow the instruction.

Solar cell A cell used to generate electricity from sunlight.

Tacho An instrument for measuring velocity, used in a car to measure the rate of revolution of the engine.

Tactile sensor A *sensor* which gives a sense of touch.

Transmitter A device for sending information, generally through the air.

Ultrasonic sensor A *sensor* which picks up sound waves which cannot be heard by the human ear.

Voice recognition The ability to recognise patterns of human speech. Some robots can recognise simple words and phrases and can then react appropriately.

Voice synthesis The ability to generate speech which can be understood by humans.

Robot books

Just Look at Robotics, Mark Lambert, Macdonald, 1985.

Robots, Hilary Henson, Kingfisher, 1981.

How it Works – The Computer, Ladybird, 1979. (Describes what computers do and how.)

Robots, Heinz Kurth, World's Work, 1983.

Science in Action: Robots, Peter Marsh, Kingfisher, 1983.

For some good stories about robots, try:
I Robot, and *The Rest of Robots*, both by Isaac Asimov, Panther books.

If you would like to build your own robot at home, try:
Robotics, Tony Potter and Ivor Guild, Usborne, 1983.
DIY Robotics and Sensors, John Billingsley, Sunshine, 1984.

There are a number of computer magazines which have articles on robots. Specialist robot magazines include:
Practical Robotics, a bi-monthly magazine, published by ECC Publications Ltd, 196–200 Balls Pond Road, Islington, London N1 4AQ
Your Robot, a monthly magazine published by EMAP, 155 Farringdon Road, London EC1R 3AD
Practical Automation, published by Industrial Press, a division of Business Press, International Limited, Quadrant House, Sutton, Surrey SM2 5AS (for companies using robots, or introducing them into the factory.)

Robot addresses

The British Robot Association, 35–39 High Street, Kempston Road, Bedford MK42 7BT (Helps to promote the use of robots in industry.)

Robot manufacturers:
Unimation, Unit C, Stafford Park 18, Telford, Shropshire, TF3 3AX (Makers of the Puma Series.)
Lamberton Robotics Limited, 26 Gartsherrie Road, Coatbridge, Strathclyde, Scotland ML5 2DL
Commotion, 241 Green Street, Enfield, Middlesex, EN3 7SJ (Makers of the Beastie.)

Computer words

Introduction

BASIC is the language most commonly used by microcomputers. The word comes from the first letters of the phrase, Beginners All-purpose Symbolic Instruction Code. BASIC is high level language because it uses words similar to human language. Different makes of microcomputer operate different dialects of BASIC. This means that programs written for one make of machine will not always run on another make.

The BASIC language contains commands and statements. These are recognized by the computer because they use special words, called *keywords*. *Commands* are typed in at the keyboard and are obeyed immediately. *Statements* are instructions for the computer that can be stored in the computer's memory in the form of a *program*. They are obeyed when the program is run. A program is a series of lines, each with a line number followed by a BASIC statement. You can have more than one statement on a line if they are separated by a colon (:). When the program is run the statements are obeyed in the same order as the line numbers (although some statements can make the computer repeat or jump over lines in the program).

For the program to do its job properly it must have the right information available, and this information is called *data*. If you wrote a program to draw a straight line between any two points then the computer would have to be given the positions of the start and the end of the line. These two positions would be the data for the program. Either the computer can ask for data with the INPUT statement, or the data could be stored in the program as DATA statements.

After you have typed a program into the computer's memory you will need some way of keeping it after the power is switched off. This is done by storing the program on to cassette or disc in the form of a *file*. So that you can have more than one program stored on cassette or disc, each file has to be given a *filename* to tell them apart.

Computers can be programmed to do many different tasks. A *database* program is rather like a card index that allows you to store facts about a subject. The facts can be sorted and related to each other, and then printed out, by operating a program which uses the database. For example, a typical database could have the size, strength, speed and accuracy of different industrial robots. Using a database program you could find out which robot could move heavy objects with the greatest speed and accuracy.

A *simulation* program attempts to show on a computer what happens during a real event. Events in the real world are usually much too complicated for a microcomputer, so computer simulations are simpler than the things they are trying to copy. Think about what happens when you pick up an apple and compare that with the RobotArm program in this book – you will soon see what we mean.

A simulation program often uses *animation*. This is a way of making an object appear to move across the screen by rapidly erasing and then drawing it in a slightly different position. This is just like how cartoon films work.

Commands

SAVE Tells the computer to save the program in the computer on tape or disc. The program must be given a filename of up to 10 characters for tape. The filename must be enclosed in inverted commas. For example, SAVE "DESIGN"

LOAD This is the opposite of SAVE. It will load a program into the computer from either tape or disc. Programs are selected by their filename. For example, LOAD "DESIGN". If you leave out the filename, and just type LOAD "" the next program will be loaded from tape, regardless of its filename.

RUN This tells the computer to start obeying the program stored in its memory.

CHAIN This command first loads a program and then runs it automatically. The program is chosen by its filename. For example, CHAIN "DESIGN". If you just type CHAIN "" the next program on the tape will be loaded and run.

LIST This allows you to look in the computer's memory. If you want to look at the program one part at a time press CNTRL and N (at the same time) and then type LIST. You will have to press SHIFT to see the next part of the program. To look at the program between lines 200 and 300 you would have to type LIST 200,300.

RENUMBER This command will renumber your program making the first line 10, the second 20, and so on. RENUMBER 900 will renumber your program starting at line 900.

DELETE You would use this command to delete a line, or group of lines, from a program. For example, DELETE 60,90 would remove all lines from 60 to 90 inclusive.

Variable names

The computer can store numbers and words in its memory. So that a program doesn't lose track of everything it has stored it uses *variables*. Suppose we wanted to use a computer to count the number of people in a room. We could use a variable called PEOPLE, and if there were eleven we could put PEOPLE=11. If somebody left the room we could change the value of people: PEOPLE=PEOPLE−1. In this example PEOPLE is called a *variable name*. If we only want to store whole numbers we use the special symbol % at the end of the variable name: PATTERNNUMBER%=2. To store words we use the special symbol $ at the end of the variable name: ROBOT$= "HERO" (note how you have to put the word in between inverted commas).

BASIC statements

INPUT Way of asking for information to be entered whilst the program is running. For example: INPUT "How old are you",AGE

PRINT Allows the program to put messages or the results of calculations on to the screen. For example: PRINT "In ten years you will be",AGE+10. PRINT by itself leaves a blank line.

MOVE Moves the graphics cursor to a new position on the screen without drawing anything: MOVE 100,250

DRAW Draws a line from the position of the graphics cursor to a new position: DRAW 325,350

COLOUR A statement which selects the colour for both the text and its background as displayed on the screen: COLOUR 1

GCOL This sets the colour of all the graphics drawn afterwards in a program: GCOL 0,2

CLS A statement which clears the text window. The text window may not be the same as the graphics window.

CLG A statement which clears the graphics window.

DIM Tells the computer to set up an array. An array is like a street of numbered houses. Something can be stored at each number.

REM This allows you to put comments into a program, saying what it does or how a part of it works. The computer ignores everything that appears after a REM. For example, in the program MindRead, REM Now we have 2X reminds us that we have doubled the number x.

MODE A statement which selects the amount of graphics and text allowed on the screen.

VDU If it is followed by a number this statement just prints the corresponding character. But certain numbers have special effects. VDU23 is used for user defined characters. VDU5 writes text at the graphics cursor, and VDU4 switches back to writing text at the text cursor. VDU7 makes a short beep. VDU24 defines the graphics window and VDU28 the text window.

DEFPROC This marks the start of procedure definition. The procedure is given a name which indicates what it does. The end of the procedure is marked by the keyword ENDPROC.

END This keyword tells the computer that it has reached the end of the program.

Index

PRINTED IN BELGIUM BY
proost
INTERNATIONAL BOOK PRODUCTION